Contributions of the Committee on Desert and Arid Zones
Research
of the Southwestern and Rocky Mountain Division of the
American Association for the Advancement of Science

Previous Symposia of the Series

1. *Climate and Man in the Southwest.* University of Arizona, Tucson, Arizona. Terah L. Smiley, editor. 1957
2. *Bioecology of the Arid and Semiarid Lands of the Southwest.* New Mexico Highlands University, Las Vegas, New Mexico. Lora M. Shields and J. Linton Gardner, editors. 1958
3. *Agricultural Problems in Arid and Semiarid Environments.* University of Wyoming, Laramie, Wyoming. Alan A. Bettle, editor. 1959
4. *Water Yield in Relation to Environment in the Southwestern United States.* Sul Ross College, Alpine, Texas. Barton H. Warnock and J. Linton Gardner, editors. 1960
5. *Ecology of Groundwater in the Southwestern United States.* Arizona State University, Tempe, Arizona. Joel E. Fletcher, editor. 1961
6. *Water Improvement.* American Association for the Advancement of Science, Denver, Colorado, J. A. Schufle and Joel E. Fletcher, editors. 1961
7. *Indian and Spanish-American Adjustments to Arid and Semiarid Environments.* Texas Technological College, Lubbock, Texas. Clark S. Knowlton, editor. 1964
8. *Native Plants and Animals as Resources in Arid Land of the Southwestern United States.* Arizona State College, Flagstaff, Arizona. Gordon L. Bender, editor. 1965
9. *Social Research in North American Moisture-Deficient Regions.* New Mexico State University, Las Cruces, New Mexico. John W. Bennett, editor. 1966
10. *Water Supplies for Arid Regions.* University of Arizona, Tucson, Arizona. J. Linton Gardner and Lloyd E. Myers, editors. 1967
11. *International Water Law Along the Mexican-American Border.* University of Texas at El Paso, Texas. Clark S. Knowlton, editor. 1968
12. *Future Environments of Arid Regions of the Southwest.* Colorado College, Colorado Springs, Colorado. Gordon L. Bender, editor. 1969
13. *Saline Water.* American Association for the Advancement of Science, New Mexico Highlands University, Las Vegas, New Mexico, Richard B. Mattox, editor. 1970
14. *Health Related Problems in Arid Lands.* Arizona State University, Tempe, Arizona, M. L. Riedesel, editor. 1971
15. *The High Plains: Problems in a Semiarid Environment.* Colorado State University, Fort Collins, Colorado. Donald D. MacPhail, editor. 1972
16. *Responses to the Dilemma: Environmental Quality vs. Economic Development.* Texas Tech University, Lubbock, Texas, William A. Dick-Peddie, editor. 1973
17. *The Reclamation of Disturbed Arid Lands.* American Association for the Advancement of Science, Denver, Colorado, Robert A. Wright, editor. 1978
18. *Energy Resource Recovery in Arid Lands.* Fort Lewis College, Durango, Colorado. K. D. Timmerhaus, editor. 1979
19. *Arid Land Plant Resources.* Texas Tech University, Lubbock, Texas. J. R. Goodin and D. Northington, editors. 1979
20. *Origin and Evolution of Deserts.* Las Vegas, Nevada, and Lubbock, Texas. Stephen G. Wells and Donald R. Haragan, editors. 1983

Pattern and Process
in Desert Ecosystems

The Committee on Desert and Arid Zones Research of the Southwestern and Rocky Mountain Division of the American Association for the Advancement of Science Statement of Purpose

The objective of the Committee on Desert and Arid Zones Research is to encourage the study of phenomena relating to and affected by human occupation of arid and semiarid regions, primarily within the areas represented by the Southwestern and Rocky Mountain Division of the A.A.A.S. This goal involves educational and research activities, both fundamental and applied, that may further understanding and efficient use of our arid lands.

Chairman: Gordon V. Johnson
Secretary: Walter G. Whitford

Dr. Bruce Buchanan
Department of Agronomy
Box 3Q
New Mexico State University
Las Cruces, NM 88003

Dr. Robert M. Chew
Box 147
Portal, AZ 85632

Dr. Clifford S. Crawford
Department of Biology
University of New Mexico
Albuquerque, NM 87131

Dr. C. Edward Freeman
Department of Biology
University of Texas at El Paso
El Paso, TX 79902

Dr. David L. Galat
Department of Zoology
Arizona State University
Tempe, AZ 85287

Dr. Donald R. Haragan
Department of Geosciences
Texas Tech University
Lubbock, TX 79409

Dr. Gordon V. Johnson
Department of Biology
University of New Mexico
Albuquerque, NM 87131

Dr. John L. Thames
School of Renewable Natural Resources
University of Arizona
Tucson, AZ 85721

Dr. Walter G. Whitford
Department of Biology
Box 3AF
New Mexico State University
Las Cruces, NM 88003

Mailing Address

Dr. M. Michelle Balcomb, Executive Officer
SWARM/AAAS
Colorado Mountain College
300 County Road 114
Glenwood Springs, CO 81601-9990

Pattern and Process in Desert Ecosystems

Edited by

W. G. Whitford

University of New Mexico Press

Albuquerque

Library of Congress Cataloging in Publication Data
Main entry under title:

Pattern and process in desert ecosystems.

   Includes bibliographies.
   1. Desert ecology.   I. Whitford, W. G.
(Walter G.), 1936–
QH541.5.D4P38   1986   574.5′2652   85–31815
ISBN 0-8263-0871-6
ISBN 0-8263-0872-4 (pbk.)

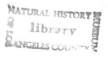

Contents

Figures

Tables

PREFACE

ECOSYSTEM ANALOGS OF
ANATOMY AND PHYSIOLOGY

Walter G. Whitford

New Mexico State University
Las Cruces, New Mexico

Depending upon which author is writing, the textbook definition of ecosystem varies: "all of the organisms and environments in a single location" (McNaughton and Wolf 1979); "all populations in a given area and the nonliving environment functioning together as a system" (Odum 1983); however, all definitions include the organisms and abiotic environment of an area. Ecologists approach the study of ecosystems in several ways. Community ecologists address questions of pattern among assemblages of organisms in ecosystems. They invoke the abiotic environment, in a general way, as a regulator of the availability or quantity of resources. Ecosystem ecologists have often focused on the flow of energy through the various trophic levels of a system or on the cycling of nutrients. These approaches focus on pools of nutrients, water availability, temperature, and light effects; hence, they provide more emphasis on abiotic parameters than exhibited by community ecologists.

Within these general approaches to the study of ecosystems are many specific questions and hypotheses that require testing.

An important goal of ecosystem science is to learn what degree of generalization can be made across ecosystems—that is, between forests, grasslands, deserts, or even among ecosystems of a single type, such as Old World versus New World deserts. Many of the general kinds of comparisons cannot be made because of different levels of knowledge about ecosystems. For example, there is considerably more information on the components of deciduous forest ecosystems than on desert ecosystems. Specifically, for example, the soil-litter arthropod fauna of eastern U.S. deciduous forests is fairly well known, while that of southwestern U.S. arid ecosystems is poorly known and many species are undescribed. The biota of the world's desert areas is generally less well known than that of more mesic systems, with the exception of tropical rain forests. The gaps in our knowledge allow comparisons of only the better known groups of organisms, as will be evident in subsequent chapters.

It is instructive to compare ecological science with medical science in order to see where we are in our understanding and approaches to the study of ecosystems. For some ecosystems, we can provide a fair description of the gross anatomy. That is, we can identify the primary producers to species and know the relative abundances of these species. We can identify the vertebrate consumers and some of the invertebrate consumers and know something about their relative abundances. We know little about the microflora and microfauna except that they are present, although some important groups like nitrogen fixers are known. Thus, our knowledge of the gross anatomy of an ecosystem is like knowing the bones, muscles, and major internal organs by name and something of their function but recognizing the endocrine glands and nervous system only as being present and important but with little or no understanding of the relationship of these parts to the skeleton, muscles, and larger internal organs.

It should, therefore, be obvious that if this is the level of our knowledge of the gross anatomy of an ecosystem our understanding of its physiology will undoubtedly be primitive. Desert ecosystems are, in general, less well known than forests or grasslands. Most research in deserts has concentrated on the physiological adaptations of organisms to the extremes of heat and lack of water. Much of our thinking about arid and semiarid ecosystems has been influenced by these kinds of studies.

Studies of desert ecosystems and ecosystem processes received a strong impetus from the International Biological Program (IBP) desert program that focused on four North American desert sites. The data from these studies are discussed in this book in the perspective of the additional information available from studies since the end of the US/IBP Desert Biome Program. To date, much of the work on deserts has been descriptive. As pointed out earlier, we are still describing the gross anatomical relationships of desert ecosystems; hence, much work must necessarily be of a descriptive nature. Understanding the anatomical relationships of desert ecosystems is further complicated by temporal changes in the relative sizes (abundances) of component parts. We have few long-term studies upon which to base questions of functional relationships of component parts. These issues are discussed with appropriate examples by the authors of contributions in this volume.

In the title of this volume, the term *pattern* refers not only to the structure or anatomy of desert systems but also to similarities and differences in responses of the components to variation in climate variables, the driving variables of the system. If we are to really understand arid and semiarid ecosystems, it is not enough to be able to predict that given x amount of rainfall in this season the numbers and biomass of rodents will double or plant biomass will double; we must know why they double. We must use our knowledge of anatomy and the attributes of the known parts to design experiments that will provide such answers and give insights into the mechanisms. In short, we must develop techniques for studying the physiology, the processes of the system.

Studies of processes in ecosystems are not very different from the classical "physiological" experiments of the early decades of the twentieth century. In order to discover what a thyroid gland does, early endocrinologists surgically removed thyroid glands from one group of animals, sham-operated another group, and compared the physiological responses. In ecological studies, removal of a predator, reducing the population of one species or group of species of potential competitors, or eliminating one or more groups of consumers is in many ways analogous to the early animal physiology studies. The following chapters provide examples of such experiments that have been and are being conducted in deserts. The studies referred to in the subsequent chapters are examples of the kinds of field studies that are needed if we are to understand the workings of desert ecosystems.

While field experiments provide one kind of data and insight into ecosystem processes, other approaches provide equally valuable information. The development of computer simulation models of functional parts of ecosystems has proven to be a useful tool in (1) synthesizing the available data on a process or processes, (2) identifying those components of the system that are most important or sensitive to manipulation and/or experimentation, and (3) generating testable hypotheses based on what is known and the current understanding of the system. The chapter by Reynolds provides an excellent example of this approach.

The purpose of holding a symposium on desert ecosystems and of publishing this volume was to provide an overview of the kinds of ongoing research that are providing the framework for understanding patterns and processes in desert ecosystems. The authors did not intend for this volume to be a complete review of all studies that could contribute to an understanding of desert ecosystems. Rather, it was our design to provide examples of how some of the important questions about desert ecosystems are being answered and how a small group of students of desert ecology and desert ecosystems perceive patterns and processes. We hope that this volume will provide a stimulus to researchers who wish to study some aspect of desert ecosystem ecology and that it will provide questions and examples of approaches that will be refined by future workers.

REFERENCES

McNaughton, S. J., and L. L. Wolf. 1979. General ecology. 2d ed. Holt, Rinehart and Winston, New York.

Odum, E. P. 1983. Basic ecology. Saunders College Publishing, New York.

1

PRIMARY PRODUCTION VARIABILITY IN DESERT ECOSYSTEMS

John A. Ludwig

New Mexico State University
Las Cruces, New Mexico

INTRODUCTION

Within regions of desert climates, it is reasonably assumed that primary production is low due to limited water availability. Compared to other major ecosystems in the biosphere, Whittaker and Likens (1973) suggest a mean net primary production for desert scrub communities of 70 g $m^{-2}yr^{-1}$ (Table 1), with extreme deserts having a mean of 3 g $m^{-2}yr^{-1}$. Lieth (1973) reports the same means, but adds the ranges of from 10 to 250 g $m^{-2}yr^{-1}$ and from 0 to 10 g $m^{-2}yr^{-1}$ for desert scrub and extreme deserts, respectively. In an extensive review of desert environments and primary production, Noy-Meir (1973) indicates a range in annual above-ground net primary production (AAGNPP) from 3 to 300 g $m^{-2}yr^{-1}$.

These reviews hint at the variations in primary production to be found in desert ecosystems, but only the recent summary by Hadley and Szarek (1981) suggests the real magnitude of these variations. Relying on more recent International Biological Program, Desert Biome (IBP/DB) studies, they report a range in AAGNPP from 2.6 to 816 g $m^{-2}yr^{-1}$.

The primary objective of this paper is to report and discuss variations in AAGNPP of deserts. Specific objectives are related to a number of questions. What ecosystem types within and between deserts have the greatest variations in AAGNPP? Under what environmental conditions are highs and lows observed? Are factors other than water availability limiting ANPP in deserts? What is the probable contribution of belowground production to total annual net primary production (ANPP)?

Before discussing these questions, I will first attempt to precisely

5

John A. Ludwig

Table 1.1. Net annual primary production for selected major ecosystems of the world (after Lieth 1973). Means and ranges in g m^{-2}yr^{-1}.

Ecosystem	Mean	Range
Tropical Rain Forest	2,000	1,000–3,500
Temperate Forest	1,000	600–1,500
Boreal Forest	500	200–1,500
Woodland	600	200–1,000
Desert Scrub	70	10–250
Extreme Desert	3	0–10

define what I mean by primary production. Then, I will present a brief history of primary production studies in deserts, pointing out the recentness of such studies. I will also discuss the methodological difficulties in measuring ANPP in deserts, which largely explains the paucity of primary production studies in deserts.

PRIMARY PRODUCTION DEFINED

Primary production is defined as the rate of organic matter (biomass) accumulation. It is the result of the net energy captured by photosynthesis that is assimilated into protoplasm per unit of surface area per unit of time (Lieth 1973). Primary production units are typically grams per meter square per year (g m^{-2}yr^{-1}), kilograms per hectare per year (kg ha^{-1}yr^{-1}), or pounds per acre per year (lb ac^{-1}yr^{-1}). Other units of time commonly used include per day (da), per week (wk), per month (mo), or per growing season (gs). As defined, production is a rate and is not to be confused with standing-crop biomass, which is often used to estimate production. Standing-crop live biomass is the organic matter existing at a given time within a given area. It reflects herbivore consumption and other losses.

HISTORY OF PRIMARY PRODUCTION STUDIES

Lieth (1973) reviews the history of production studies for our biosphere. Although there was a vague concept of energy capture that can be traced back to Aristotle, the first measurements of production were done in forests and agricultural fields in the 1860s. These first production studies provided the first realization that natural forests are more productive than the crops in fields embedded within these forests.

The history of primary production studies in deserts of North America can be divided into those before 1970 (pre-IBP/DB) and those after 1970. In the Chihuahuan Desert the pre-IBP/DB productivity studies of Chew and Chew (1965) and Burk and Dick-Peddie (1973) suggest an AAGNPP in the range of 50–100 g m^{-2}yr^{-1} for creosotebush, *Larrea tridentata*, ecosystems. In the Great Basin Desert, Pearson (1965) reports a AAGNPP of about 125 g m^{-2}yr^{-1}. For Mojave Desert sites, AAGNPP varies from 0 to 62 g m^{-2}yr^{-1} (Beatley 1969).

During the IBP/DB studies, different desert ecologists were involved in primary production measurements in each of the major deserts of North America. Results for these studies have been summarized by Hadley and Szarek (1981) and Webb et al. (1983). Additional studies will be reported later in this paper.

After the IBP/DB projects, AAGNPP studies have continued through various funding agencies as part of other projects. For example, the Department of Energy (DOE) funded some productivity studies as part of their Waste Isolation Pilot Plant (WIPP) project in southeastern New Mexico (Ludwig and Freas 1980, Ludwig et al. 1981). The National Science Foundation (NSF) has funded some AAGNPP studies as part of a Desert Decomposition project (Parker et al. 1982) and more recently as part of the Long-Term Ecological Research (LTER) project (Whitford et al. 1982).

Primary production studies in deserts outside of (but including) North America have been recently reviewed (West 1983). An excellent summary of productivity studies in the Sahel is now available (Penning de Vries and Djiteye 1982). Such summaries are also now available for Mongolia (Kazantseva 1980), for Rajasthan, India (Sharma 1982), and for Tunisia (Floret et al. 1982). These studies will be compared later in this paper.

DESERT PRIMARY PRODUCTION METHODS

Direct-Destructive Methods. The following methods provide a direct and sometimes rapid estimate of AAGNPP, but also require that the plants (or parts thereof) being measured are destroyed in the process.

Harvesting standing crop biomass using clipped quadrats is probably the most commonly used method for estimating AAGNPP. The easiest procedure is to do a single harvest at the "peak biomass" of the growing season. However, this simple procedure is subject of a number of potential errors (Fig. 1a) as it assumes that all the standing crop produced during the season is present and that there is no accumulation present from previous years. Thus, it only provides a reasonably accurate estimate of true AAGNPP for annual plants that have a single distinct growth peak and low turnover. Although more effort, a more accurate procedure is to make multiple harvests and to sum the peaks for each species (Fig. 1b). Regardless of which harvest procedure is used, there is always some turnover and consumption by herbivores, and the quadrat harvest estimate of AAGNPP will always be low.

Harvesting individual plants whose density is estimated by a plotless distance method can also provide an estimate of AAGNPP. The point-centered quarter method uses the distance from a random point to the nearest individual plant in each of four quarters about the point to provide an estimate of the density of each plant species (Cottam and Curtis 1956). If each individual plant to which a distance measure is made is also harvested and field sorted by species, the average biomass of each species can subsequently be determined. Thus, given the density of each species and its average weight, the standing crop biomass can be calculated as: $g\ m^{-2} = g\ individual^{-1} \times individuals\ m^{-2}$. If such plotless harvests are made throughout the growing season, a reasonably accurate estimate of AAGNPP is obtained by summing the standing crop biomass peaks of the individual species.

If gas exchange apparatus is available, field measurement of net carbon dioxide uptake can be made to estimate the amount of carbon fixed by a plant. About 2.2 g dry weight plant biomass is produced from every g of carbon fixed. For an accurate estimate of production, gas exchange measurements must be made for a number of full day–night cycles throughout the growing season. Most plants are too large to measure the gas exchange for the entire plant; thus, gas exchange on a leaf area or leaf biomass basis is often used. Then, estimates of total leaf area per plant and plant density must be available to determine productivity on a $g\ m^{-2}yr^{-1}$ basis.

Indirect-Nondestructive Methods.   The following methods provide an estimate of AAGNPP using an "easily" measured plant attribute to estimate biomass through simple regression procedures. These methods are nondestructive in the sense that once the regression relationship is known between biomass and the plant attribute, the measured attribute is all that is needed to make subsequent estimates.

A one-step indirect method provides an estimate of standing-crop biomass from a single measured attribute. For example, a regression to predict $g\ m^{-2}$ given a simple measure of percentage of ground cover of a

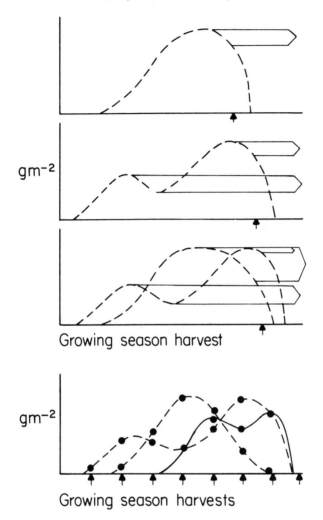

gm⁻²

Growing season harvest

gm⁻²

Growing season harvests

Figure 1.1 Estimating annual aboveground net primary production (AAGNPP) by single (a) and multiple (b) biomass harvests during the growing season.

species is such a method. If seasonal cover is dynamic and reflects biomass changes, then a series of such estimates through the growing season allows for the determination of AAGNPP by summing peaks of the species involved.

A multiple-step method requires the measurement of two or more attributes in order to predict standing crop biomass. For example, a regression to estimate g of leaf biomass from a simple measurement of shoot length can be the first step. However, an estimate of the number of shoots per plant is needed then to estimate the biomass of leaves per plant. Then, an estimate of the density of plants is needed to estimate the biomass of leaves per unit area, g leaf m^{-2} = g shoot^{-1} × shoots plant^{-1} × plants m^{-2}. Repeated estimates of shoot length, shoot number, and plant density made throughout the growing season allows for a reasonable estimate of AAGNPP by summing peaks for the species involved.

One caution in using such multistep estimation procedures is what I call the flaring errors effect (Fig. 2). If, by chance, your estimates of shoot length, shoot number, and plant density are at their upper confidence limits (UCL), your estimate of g leaf m^{-2} = 105 (0.07 g shoot^{-1} × 125 shoots plant^{-1} × plants m^{-2}). However, if your estimates are at their lower confidence limits (LCL), then your estimate of g leaf m^{-2} = 18 (0.03 g shoot^{-1} × 75 shoots plant^{-1} × 8 plants m^{-2} = 18). This extreme range in the likely estimate for leaf biomass illustrates that each of the estimates in this multistep method has its own error associated with it and that the desired answer has a multiplicative error associated with it. Of course, one trusts that with adequate sampling the central limit theorem will hold and random errors will cancel and give an answer near the true mean.

DESERT PRIMARY PRODUCTION VARIATIONS

The question of variability in AAGNPP within a given desert can be addressed by examining data from the northern Chihuahuan Desert (Table 2). The six ecosystems were part of two Jornada study sites of the IBP/DP project (Smith and Ludwig 1978). Table 2 presents AAGNPP for six years for the six very different ecosystems. The seasonal dynamics of productivity for some selected species from these ecosystems has been reported by Ludwig and Whitford (1981).

The large arroyos, which dissect the alluvial fans of the bajada site, had the greatest variability in AAGNPP—from a low of only 30 g m^{-2}yr^{-1} to a high of over 450 g m^{-2}yr^{-1}. The low AAGNPP in 1971 followed a summer and fall of 1970 with low precipitation, with 1971 having a very dry

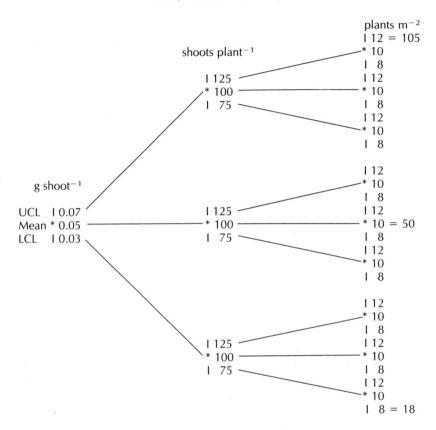

Figure 1.2 The flaring errors effect due to multiplicative errors in estimation (upper confidence limits [UCL]
and lower confidence limits [LCL]) of annual aboveground net primary production (AAGNPP) using multiple-step methods, such as dimension analysis.

winter, spring, and summer season (Table 3). The high AAGNPP in 1973
followed a summer and fall of 1972 with high precipitation, with the
winter, spring, and summer of 1973 being relatively moist.

   This large arroyo ecosystem consists of three major deep-rooted shrubs:
honey mesquite, *Prosopis glandulosa* var. *torreyana;* desert willow, *Chilopsis linearis;* and apache plume, *Fallugia paradoxa.* Each of these species
contributes significantly to AAGNPP through production of leaf, shoot, and
reproductive biomass.

Table 1.2. Annual above-ground net primary production (AAGNPP) for six northern Chihuahuan Desert ecosystems on the Jornada del Muerto, New Mexico.

| Chihuahuan Desert | AAGNPP—g m^{-2}yr^{-1} | | | | | |
Jornada Ecosystems	1970	1971	1972	1973	1974	1975
Bajada—Alluvial Fans	—	161	292	129	101	53
Bajada—Small Arroyos	—	37	97	318	179	87
Bajada—Large Arroyos	—	30	297	456	229	64
Basin—Slopes	—	48	91	179	51	—
Basin—Swales	366	592	387	292	492	—
Basin—Playa Lake	258	52	74	188	191	—

Of the six ecosystems, the swales of the basin Jornada site had the absolute highest AAGNPP—about 600 g m^{-2}yr^{-1} during 1971 of the IBP/DB years (Table 2). The low during 1973 was still about 300 g m^{-2}yr^{-1}; thus, this ecosystem had the least variability in AAGNPP. The ecosystem is dominated by tobosa grass, *Hilaria mutica,* with other grasses and forbs contributing less than 10% towards AAGNPP. This swale ecosystem is characterized by being a run-on site, with surface-flow water from the surrounding bajada and basin slopes collecting in the deep sandy-loan soils (Ludwig and Whitford 1981). Thus, even in an overall dry year (as 1972), a single summer high-intensity thunderstorm can provide sufficient run-on water to the swale for good growth of tobosa grass.

Table 1.3. Annual and seasonal precipitation patterns for the northern Chihuahuan Desert ecosystem on the Jornada del Muerto, New Mexico.

| Season | Precipitation—mm | | | | | |
	1970	1971	1972	1973	1974	1975
Winter	—	13	31	75	21	47
Spring	—	4	14	30	2	12
Summer	105	77	176	119	158	72
Fall	41	88	179	4	146	95
Annual	—	182	400	228	327	226

Table 1.4. Annual aboveground net primary production (AAGNPP) for three northern Chihuahuan Desert ecosystems on the Los Medanos DOE/WIPP site, Carlsbad, New Mexico.

Chihuahuan Desert Los Medanos Ecosystem	AAGNPP—g $m^{-2}yr^{-1}$	
	1978	1979
Creosotebush Flats	416	243
Mesquite-Grassland Mesa	23	82
Oak-Mesquite Dunes	34	394

The magnitude of variability within a desert is also illustrated by data from another northern Chihuahuan Desert area (Table 4). Three ecosystems were studied for two years as part of the DOE/WIPP project (Ludwig and Freas 1980, Ludwig et al. 1981). The creosotebush flats, dominated by *Larrea* and snakeweed, *Xanthocephalum sarothrae*, had a higher AAGNPP in 1978 than in 1979, whereas the other two ecosystems had lower values. In 1978 precipitation consisted of a number of small thunderstorms scattered throughout the summer and fall. The shallow, diffusely rooted creosotebush is capable of taking advantage of such rainfall pattern (Ludwig 1977). The deep-rooted mesquite and oak, *Quercus harvardii*, have much higher productivity when soils are moist to a deep depth, as with the winter rains of 1979. AAGNPP in the oak-mesquite dunes increased in 1979 to over ten times that of 1978.

The question of variability in AAGNPP between different deserts can be addressed by examining summary data from a variety of study sites (Table 5). A comparison of a dry year (1972) with a wet year (1973) in the northern Mojave Desert suggests a threefold increase in AAGNPP (Bamberg et al. 1976). A similar comparison for winter annuals in the Sonoran Desert (Patten 1978) indicates about a tenfold increase in AAGNPP during a wet winter (1972–73) over a drier winter (1973–74). A comparison of a dry year (1963) with a wetter year (1964) at three sites in the Negev Desert of Israel suggests about a fivefold increase at two sites and about a fourfold increase at the other site (Orshan and Diskin 1968).

The AAGNPP of summer ephemerals varied about fivefold between four different sites in the Rajasthan desert of India (Sharma 1982). Ex-

Table 1.5. Annual aboveground net primary production (AAGNPP) in different desert ecosystems during different years.

Desert	Ecosystem	Year	$g\ m^{-2}yr$ AAGNPP	Reference
Mojave	Larrea-Ambrosia-Lycium	1972	13	Bamberg et al.
USA		1973	44	1976
Sonoran	Winter Ephemerals within	1973	95	Patten
USA	Larrea-Cercidium	1974	9	1978
Negev	Artemisietum herbae-albae	1963	4	Orshan and
Israel		1964	20	Diskin 1968
	Zygophylletum dumosi	1963	4	
		1964	20	
	Anabasidetum articulati	1963	12	
		1964	43	
Rajasthan	Summer Ephemerals—Site I	1972	50	Sharma
India	—Site II	1972	126	1982
	—Site III	1972	51	
	—Site IV	1972	20	
Gobi	Haloxylon-Ephedra—Hammada	1978	0	Kazantseva
Mongolia	—Gullies	1978	155	1980
	Iljinia-Haloxylon—Hammada	1978	1	
	—Gullies	1978	6	
	Nitraria-Reaumuria—Hammada	1978	22	
	Haloxylon-Artemisia—Hammada	1978	28	
	—Gullies	1978	145	
	Sympegma-Reaumuria—Hammada	1978	29	
	—Gullies	1978	48	
Pre-Sahara	Rhantherium—on deep sands	1972	102	Floret et al.
Tunisia		1973	116	1982
		1974	106	
		1975	101	
		1976	155	
		1977	22	

treme variability was found between different sites in the Gobi Desert of Mongolia, with AAGNPP being higher in gullies (dry-beds, washes, arroyos) than on the hammadas (dry-bed divides, uplands, flats, fans) between the gullies due to water run-on (Kazantseva 1980). On a single site in the pre-Sahara of Tunisia, AAGNPP varied about sixfold between peak production in the spring of 1976 compared to the spring of 1977, although the other four years were relatively constant.

DISCUSSION AND CONCLUSIONS

From the comparisons of AAGNPP between different ecosystems within deserts and between deserts, it is clear that the position of an ecosystem relative to patterns of water run-on and run-off in the landscape and the soil water storage capacity of the system largely determines potential primary productivity. Because patterns of precipitation are highly varied from year to year, the potential effectiveness of precipitation in providing water inputs to a given ecosystem are themselves highly varied. This results in a highly variable level of AAGNPP from year to year within any given desert ecosystem and between different ecosystems within a desert area.

The above results and discussion tends to emphasize the importance of water to desert ecosystems. However, recent studies suggest that other factors, such as soil nutrients, may also limit primary production (Penning de Vries and Djiteye 1982). Their results from a north–south transect across the Sahel suggest that as precipitation exceeds 200 mm, the level of primary production does not reach that expected. Their results indicate that nitrogen and phosphorus limit productivity in deserts at higher levels of water input. A limitation of nitrogen to primary production in our northern Chihuahuan Desert has also been reported (Ettershank et al. 1978). There has also been a suggestion that mycorrhizal relations may limit productivity in arid and semiarid ecosystems (Trappe 1981).

The results reported in this paper are for annual aboveground net primary productivity (AAGNPP). Total annual net primary production (ANPP) must include the assimilation of energy into the biomass of the root systems of the plants within the ecosystem. The determination of such belowground net primary production values is extremely difficult, with the gas exchange method discussed earlier serving as one technique for obtaining such estimates. A comparison of harvest measurements for AAGNPP and gas exchange measurements suggest that ANPP is about three times AAGNPP for Mojave Desert shrubs (Bamberg et al. 1976). The use of radioactive carbon has also been used to estimate the partitioning of fixed CO_2 between aboveground and belowground plant parts (Wallace et al. 1980). Data for root-to-shoot ratios for desert shrubs indicate a highly variable pattern of final biomass accumulation (Ludwig 1977, Barbour 1973, Noy-Meir 1973).

In conclusion, there is greater variability between different ecosystems within a desert than between many different deserts. There is also great variability between different years within a given desert ecosystem. These variations are largely related to patterns of water run-on and run-off in relation to potential soil water storage of the different desert ecosystems.

16   *John A. Ludwig*

REFERENCES

Bamberg, S. A., A. T. Vollmer, G. E. Klienkopf, and T. L. Ackerman. 1976. A comparison of seasonal primary production of Mojave Desert shrubs during wet and dry years. American Midland Naturalist 95:398–405.

Barbour, M. G. 1973. Desert dogma reexamined: root/shoot productivity and plant spacing. American Midland Naturalist 89:41–57.

Beatley, J. C. 1969. Biomass of desert winter annual populations in southern Nevada. Oikos 20:261–273.

Burk, J. H., and W. A. Dick-Peddie. 1973. Comparative production of *Larrea divaricata* Cav. on three geomorphic surfaces in southern New Mexico. Ecology 54:1094–1102.

Chew, R. M., and A. E. Chew. 1965. The primary productivity of a desert shrub (*Larrea tridentata*) community. Ecological Monographs 35:355–375.

Cottom, G., and J. T. Curtis. 1956. The use of distance measures in phytosociological sampling. Ecology 37:451–460.

Ettershank, G., J. A. Ettershank, M. Bryant and W. G. Whitford. 1978. Effects of nitrogen fertilization on primary production in a Chihuahuan Desert ecosystem. Journal of Arid Environments 1:135–139.

Floret, C., R. Pontanier, and S. Rambal. 1982. Measurement and modelling of primary production and water use in a south Tunisian steppe. Journal of Arid Environments 5:77–90.

Hadley, N. F., and S. R. Szarek. 1981. Productivity of desert ecosystems. BioScience 31:747–753.

Kazantseva, T. I. 1980. Productivity and dynamics of the above-ground biomass of desert plants, pp. 76–84. *In:* Problemy Osvoeiya Pustyn, No. 2., Komarov Botanical Institute, Academy of Science of the USSR.

Lieth, H. 1973. Primary production: Terrestrial ecosystems. Human Ecology 1:303–332.

Ludwig, J. A. 1977. Distributional adaptations of root systems in desert environments, pp. 85–91. *In:* J. K. Marshall (ed.). the belowground ecosystem symposium: A synthesis of plant-associated processes. Range Science Department Science Series Number 26, Colorado State University, Fort Collins, Colorado.

Ludwig, J. A., and K. E. Freas. 1980. Primary production patterns on the Los Medanos WIPP study area for 1978, pp. 215–224. *In:* T. L. Best and S. Neuhauser (eds.). A report of biological investigations at the Los Medanos Waste Isolation Pilot Plant (WIPP) area of New Mexico during FY1978. Sandia Laboratories, Albuquerque, New Mexico.

Ludwig, J. A., J. Honea, and B. Barber. 1981. Primary production patterns on the Los Medanos WIPP study area for 1979. A report of biological investigations at the Los Medanos Waste Isolation Pilot Plant (WIPP) area of New Mexico during FY1979. Sandia Laboratories, Albuquerque, New Mexico.

Ludwig, J. A., and W. G. Whitford. 1981. Short-term water and energy flow in arid ecosystems, pp. 271–299. *In:* D. W. Goodall and R. A. Perry (eds.). Arid land ecosystems: Structure, functioning and management. Vol. 2. International Biological Programme No. 17, Cambridge University Press, London.

Noy-Meir, I. 1973. Desert ecosystems: environment and producers. Annual Reviews of Ecology and Systematics 4:25–51.

Orshan, G., and S. Diskin. 1968. Seasonal changes in productivity under desert conditions, pp. 191–201. *In:* F. E. Echardt (ed.). Functioning of terrestrial ecosystems at the primary production level. Proceedings of the Copenhagen Symposium, UNESCO, Paris.

Parker, L. W., H. G. Fowler, G. Ettershank, and W. G. Whitford. 1982. The effects of subterranean removal on desert soil nitrogen and ephemeral flora. Journal of Arid Environments 5:53–59.

Patten, D. T. 1978. Productivity and production efficiency of an upper Sonoran Desert ephemeral community. American Journal of Botany 65:891–895.

Pearson, L. C. 1965. Primary productivity in grazed and ungrazed desert communities of eastern Idaho. Ecology 46:278–285.

Penning de Vries, F. W. T., and M. A. Djiteye (eds.). 1982. La productivite des paturages Saheliens. Centre for Agricultural Publication and Documentation, Wageningen, Netherlands.

Sharma, B. M. 1982. Plant biomass in the semi-arid zone of India. Journal of Arid Environments 5:29–33.

Smith, S. D., and J. A. Ludwig. 1978. The distribution and phytosociology of *Yucca elata* in southern New Mexico. American Midland Naturalist 100:202–212.

Trappe, J. M. 1981. Mycorrhizae and productivity of arid and semiarid rangelands, pp. 581–599. *In:* Advances in food producing systems for arid and semiarid lands. Academic Press, New York.

Wallace, A., R. T. Mueller, J. W. Cha, and E. M. Romney. 1980. 14-C distribution in roots following photosynthesis of the label in perennial plants in the northern Mojave Desert. Great Basin Naturalist Memoirs 4:177–191.

Webb, W. L., W. K. Lauenroth, S. R. Szarek, and R. S. Kinerson. 1983. Primary production and abiotic controls in forests, grasslands, and desert ecosystems in the United States. Ecology 64:134–151.

West, N. E. 1983. Overview of North American temperate deserts and semideserts, pp. 321–330. *In:* N. E. West (ed.). Temperate Deserts and Semi-Deserts. Elsevier Scientific Publ. Co., Amsterdam.

Whitford, W. G., G. Cunningham, W. Conley, P. Wierenga, M. Hussain, and J. Ludwig. 1982. The Jornada NMSU Range LTER site. Bulletin of the Ecological Society 63:117 (Abstract).

Whittaker, R. H., and G. E. Likens. 1973. Primary production: The biosphere and man. Human Ecology 1:357–369.

2

ADAPTATIVE STRATEGIES OF DESERT SHRUBS WITH SPECIAL REFERENCE TO THE CREOSOTEBUSH
(*Larrea tridentata* [DC] Cov.)

James F. Reynolds

North Carolina State University
Raleigh, North Carolina

INTRODUCTION

In spite of the numerous studies undertaken to elucidate the biology of the creosotebush (*Larrea tridentata* [DC] Cov.), this important shrub of the North American deserts remains somewhat of an ecological enigma. To date, no functional description of its physiological ecology can fully explain the observed year-to-year variations in its vegetative and reproductive growth dynamics or clarify the relative importance of those environmental factors which control crucial primary productivity processes. In conjunction with experimentation, I believe that mathematical models of plant growth will play an important role in the eventual realization of such a functional description for *Larrea*. However, to be helpful, such models must be designed in a way to increase our understanding of the integrated nature of the adaptive strategy of the species. The modeling research on *Larrea* that Gary Cunningham of New Mexico State University and I have initiated (see Cunningham and Reynolds 1978, Reynolds et al. 1980, Reynolds and Cunningham 1981) is a first, albeit preliminary, step toward the development of this type of model. In this paper, my objective is, first, to discuss the biology of the creosotebush in terms of a static definition of its adaptive strategy, and, second, to present an overview of the approach that we're using to model the dynamic features of the adaptive strategy of *Larrea* in the Chihuahuan Desert. The value of the approach for hypothesis testing will be evaluated with regard to its potential as a tool for increasing our understanding of plant adaptations in arid environments.

STRATEGIES

Three Primary Models

The intent of this detailed (IBP) study of *Larrea* is . . . to delimit specifically what strategies are used [by this shrub].—Solbrig (1977)

While ecologists commonly use the term *strategy* in referring to how plants are adapted to their environment, there are numerous and varied ways of viewing a plant strategy, ranging from population characteristics and life histories to morphological and physiological traits (Grime 1982). In view of this, Grime (1977, 1979) developed a valuable pedagogical model for conceptualizing plant strategies. Grime classified external factors that effectively limit plant biomass in any habitat into two categories: stress and disturbance. Stress includes factors that restrict primary productivity, such as extremes of temperature, shortages of light, water, nutrients, and so forth. Disturbance involves the partial or total destruction of plant biomass by herbivory, fire, trampling, pathogens, and so forth. On the basis of the various combinations of high and low stress with high and low disturbance, Grime identified three primary plant strategies* that have evolved in response to these external factors: *competitive* (low stress with low disturbance), *stress-tolerant* (high stress with low disturbance), and *ruderal* (low stress with high disturbance). Each of these strategies is characterized by a set of traits which contribute to the overall success of an organism in meeting the demands of its particular environment; a brief summary of some characteristics associated with each strategy is given in Table 2.1.

In desert ecosystems, where shortage of resources (for example, water and nutrients) and environmental extremes (for example, fluctuations in temperature and rainfall) prevail, the stress-tolerant and ruderal strategies predominate. Xerophytic shrubs, the most abundant life form in deserts (Solbrig 1977), can be classified as stress-tolerant while desert ephemerals exemplify the ruderal strategy, that is, they possess special adaptations for exploiting intermittently favorable environments (see Table 2.1). Since desert ruderals may experience varying degrees of stress during their life

---

*The high stress with high disturbance category was deemed a nonviable plant habitat.

cycle, Grime (1979) further classifies them as "stress-tolerant ruderals," illustrating that the three strategies are, of course, extremes and that any plant strategy is clearly some complex compromise that reflects a complex of environmental demands.

Larrea: A Stress-Tolerant Strategist

Despite its *remarkable* adaptation to desert climates, the creosote-bush is *unremarkable* in its dry weight and growth characteristics . . . .—Whittaker and Niering (1975) [italics added]

The ecological dominance of the creosotebush in the plant communities of the warm deserts of North America attests to its "remarkable adaptation" to arid environments. The literature on *Larrea,* including recent synthesis volumes by Mabry et al. (1977) and Compos-Lopez et al. (1979), reveals a large suite of characteristics (physiological, morphological, and others) which undoubtedly contribute to the overall success of creosote-bush in a xeric habitat. I have summarized some of these in Table 2.1 for easy comparison to the three plant strategies. As can be seen, *Larrea* fits rather well into the stress-tolerant category (see Table 2.1). Stresses that limit primary productivity in creosotebush are mainly environmental, that is, due to shortages of moisture and suboptimal temperatures; although some may be plant-induced (Grime 1979), for example, shortages in solar energy due to shading (rare?) or shortages of nutrients due to a sequestering in existing plant biomass (Reynolds and Cunningham 1981). Competition for limited resources between neighboring plants is usually considered unimportant in desert ecosystems relative to environmental constraints (Grime 1979) but may also be significant, at least during certain times of the year. Chew and Chew (1965) reported that, in some cases, the root systems of neighboring creosotebushes in a southeastern Arizona study site overlapped, suggesting that competition for soil moisture could be important; Ludwig (1977) found no such root overlap in a creosotebush community in southern New Mexico.

From Table 2.1 it can be seen that certain characteristics of the stress-tolerant strategy are structural (nondynamic, for example, leaf size) while others are functional or behavioral (dynamic, for example, the relative growth rate). Since structure and function are interdependent, the integrated behavior of a plant is determined by the nature of these relationships. For example, low photosynthesis rates in *Larrea* are, in part, a reflection of certain morphological features of xerophytic leaves (small cells, thick cell walls, and so forth) (Orians and Solbrig 1977); such

Table 2.1. General characteristics of competitive, ruderal, and stress-tolerant plants (from Grime 1977, 1979) compared to some recorded characteristics for creosotebush. Key: C=Chihuahuan Desert, S=Sonoran Desert, D=Colorado Desert of California, M=Mojave Desert

	Competitive	Ruderal	Stress-tolerant	Creosotebush (Larrea)	References
Morphology					
Life forms	Herbs, shrubs and trees	Herbs	Lichens, herbs, shrubs and trees	Perennial shrub	2
Shoot morphology	Dense canopy; extensive lateral spread above and below ground	Small stature; limited lateral spread	Extremely wide range of growth forms	Distinct growth form associated with desert; varies with soil depth (C) = relatively short (0.9 m), considerable branching (S) = relatively tall (1.4 m), moderate branching	1,2,3
Leaf form	Robust, often mesomorphic	Various, often mesomorphic	Often small or leathery, or needlelike	Small; reduced	2
Life-History					
Longevity of established phase	Long or relatively short	Very short	Long–very long	Longevity >100 years? Clone (M) >2,000–11,700 years?	1,2,4 11,14
Longevity of leaves and roots	Relatively short	Short	Long	<1–2 years (C) 1.25–1.5 years (S)	3 4
Leaf phenology	Well-defined peaks of leaf production coinciding with period(s) of maximum potential productivity	Short phase of leaf production in period of high potential productivity	Evergreens, with various patterns of leaf production	Evergreen; various patterns (often linked to moisture availability) June-November (S) (largely independent of moisture) March-October (M) April-November (C) Nodes produced throughout year (D)	4 2 6 10
Phenology of flowering	Flowers produced after (or, more rarely) before periods of maximum potential productivity	Flowers produced early in the life-history	No general relationship between flowering and season	Flowers virtually throughout year; highly dependent upon moisture, temperature	2,4,5,7,10

Proportion of annual production devoted to seeds	Small	Large	Small	Quite variable; 0.5–43% of annual aboveground production; highly dependent upon moisture conditions	2,3,5
Perennation	Dormant buds and seeds	Dormant seeds	Stress-tolerant leaves and roots	Stress-tolerant leaves (temperature and desiccation)	9,10
Physiology					
Maximum potential relative growth rate	Rapid	Rapid	Slow	"Relatively slow" but "steady"	7
Response to stress	Rapid morphogenetic response (shoot/root ratio, leaf area) maximizing vegetative growth	Rapid curtailment vegetative growth; diversion of resources into flowering	Morphogenetic responses slow and small in magnitude	Moisture-stress induced morphological variations (size, shape of leaves, tissue shedding)	2,13
Photosynthesis and mineral nutrient uptake	Strongly seasonal, coinciding with long continuous period of vegetative growth	Opportunistic, coinciding with vegetative growth	Opportunistic, often uncoupled from vegetative growth	Positive net CO_2 balance throughout year (D); able to exhibit similar photosynthesis rates during both favorable and unfavorable conditions during year; seasonal patterns of photosynthesis	2,9,10,12,13
Acclimation of photosynthesis, mineral nutrition and tissue hardiness to seasonal change in temperature, light and moisture	Weakly developed	Weakly developed	Strongly developed	Photosynthesis and respiration acclimation to temperature strongly developed	8,12,13
Storage of photosynthate, mineral nutrients	Most rapidly incorporated into structure; proportion stored forms capital for expansion of growth in the following growing season	Confined to seeds	Storage systems in leaves, stems and/or roots	Nonstructural carbon pools relatively small; storage small?	10,12

References: 1=Barbour (1969), 2=Barbour et al. (1977a), 3=Burk and Dick-Peddie, 4=Chew and Chew (1965), 5=Cunningham et al. (1979), 6=Ludwig and Flavill (1979), 7=Ludwig and Whitford (1981), 8=Mooney et al. (1977), 9=Odening et al. (1974), 10=Oechel et al. (1972), 11=Sternberg (1976), 12=Strain (1969), 13=Strain and Chase (1966), 14=Vasek (1980).

phenomena are relevant for explaining the so-called unremarkable growth characteristics of *Larrea* noted by Whittaker and Niering (1975). Identification of patterns of functional response is made difficult because of their great variability as compared to structural traits.

This description of *Larrea* as a stress-tolerant plant will serve as the static model of its strategy. Such a model can be helpful in gaining insights into patterns of adaptations. However, a dynamic model is required if an integrated understanding of strategy is to be achieved. In view of this desired goal, I'm defining plant strategy here to be the dynamic, systems-level behavior of a plant which results in the successful exploitation of a given environment; this behavior is genetically based and includes all responses (both stressed and unstressed) to the environment, particularly the allocation of resources to various functions, for example, to reproduction, assimilation, maintenance, growth, and so forth. Implied in this definition of strategy are those structural features of the plant which determine the bounds for the set of possible behaviors. A dynamic model should be able to quantify both the short- and long-term magnitudes of the contribution of each essential structure–function relationship to this overall strategy. "Contribution" refers to any controlling influence (that is, physical/chemical interactions, feedback and control mechanisms, size and shape factors, and so forth) that a trait or resulting behavior may have on the procurement, utilization, and distribution of essential elements and nutrients (including water) in the plant. Furthermore, for the model to be general, it is important that this quantification be conducted over a wide range of environmental scenarios to ensure that all significant interactions are identified and included.

Optimization and Strategies

Natural selection produces optimal results unless constrained by history or by competing goals.—Cody (1974)

The stress-tolerant strategy in *Larrea* can be considered an evolutionary design. For example, numerous features that reduce water loss (for example, thick palisade tissue, reduced leaf surface area, low stomatal conductance) are common to most xerophytic desert shrubs (Whittaker 1970), implying a similar solution to a similar problem—the minimization of water loss. In terms of strategy, a number of complex interactions exist and must be considered. The reduction of water loss in xerophytes, a necessary design problem, restricts the upper bounds of photosynthesis which, in turn, limits carbon availability for root growth and increased water uptake. It's obvious that a plant must simultaneously satisfy a number of conflicting demands, and any attempt to define a dynamic strategy must necessarily address such complexity. This is where mathematical models can play an important role.

Plant modelers are making interesting contributions to the question of the so-called optimal design of phenotypes. The essential features of some system of interest are represented in mathematical form (usually differential calculus), and the behavior of these systems of equations are examined in terms of limits and optimal solutions that maximize (or minimize) some "goal." In Table 2.2 I've summarized a number of such models to illustrate the diversity of structural and functional phenotypes that have been studied with respect to optimal solutions for meeting specific goals, such as seed production.

What a model might predict as optimum (assuming the model is justified) may not, of course, be what we observe in nature. As quoted above, Cody (1974) provides two biological explanations: (1) historical, for example, the absence of a mutation which would result in such a design, or (2) conflicting demands for limited resources. On the other hand, it is also important to realize that natural selection does not necessarily produce "optimal" phenotypes. The "best-adapted phenotype" of a species (that is, the one with the greatest contribution of a genotype to future generations) (Cody 1974) may not be the "optimal phenotype" in the absence of selective pressure. Hence, the idea that natural selection produces optimal results must be viewed cautiously. In the next section the conceptual approach for developing a dynamic model of a growth strategy is introduced.

INTEGRATION OF SHOOT AND ROOT ACTIVITIES

Functional Balance Model

. . . [A] well-adapted plant is an integrated system.—Geiger (1979)

The balance of growth at the whole-plant level is a function of the relative contribution of each plant organ. This is exemplified by the interactions between organs of the shoot with those of the root (see reviews by Mooney 1972, Wareing and Patrick 1975, Russell 1977, Thornley 1977, Fischer and Turner 1978, and Novoa and Loomis 1981). Shoot growth is dependent on certain growth substances supplied by the root, while root growth is dependent on growth substances supplied by the shoot; consequently, there is a reciprocal functional relationship between

Table 2.2. Summary of recent studies in which mathematical models have been used to examine "maximization goals" with respect to adaptive traits (tactics) of plants. In each study, the goal was explicitly defined as listed.

Maximization Goal	Tactic(s)	References
Reproductive (= seed) Yield	Energy allocation; vegetative vs. reproductive growth a. timing of reproductive growth b. duration of reproductive growth c. graded vs. priority allocation	Cohen (1968, 1971); Denholm (1975); King and Roughgarten (1982a,b; 1983); Moldau (1974, 1977); Paltridge and Denholm (1974)
Number of surviving offspring (growth of population	Life history characteristics a. iteropary vs. semelpary b. age of first reproduction c. reproductive effect (e.g., seed size) d. sexual vs. asexual reproduction	Gadgil and Bossert (1970); Hickman (1977); Hubbell and Werner (1979) Mendelssohn (1976); Schaffer and Gadgil (1975)
Whole-plant rate of net carbon gain	Leaf thickness	Givnish (1979)
Net leaf photosynthesis, transpiration efficiency, leaf energy budget	Leaf characteristics a. form b. diffusive resistances c. distribution in canopy d. leaf angles	Parkhurst and Loucks (1972); Taylor (1980)
Vegetative Yield (= mean annual carbon assimilation)	Stomatal behavior	Jones (1980)
Water-use Efficiency (carbon assimilated/water evaporated)	Temperature acclimation Stomatal behavior	Mooney (1980) Cowan and Farquhar (1977); Williams (1983); Cowan (1982)
Daily carbon gain of plant canopy	Leaf nitrogen distribution in canopy	Field (1983)
Leaf net carbon assimilation rate	Shoot:root surface area ratio	Moldau (1974)
Net carbon fixation per unit time	Shoot:root dry matter ratio	Gadgil and Gadgil (1979)
Relative growth rate (whole plant)	Shoot:root dry matter ratio	Mooney and Gulmon (1979); Reynolds and Thornley (1982)
Meeting evaporative demand of plant given specific soil moisture and root biomass	"Design" of root system a. root resistance:volume ratio b. root shape c. root size	Caldwell (1976); Fowkes and Landsberg (1981)

Table 2.3. Examples of research involving Davidson's (1969) proposed quantitative expression [eqn (1)] for the balance between shoot and root growth.

Shoot activity=carbon uptake rate; root activity=nitrogen uptake rate
  Shribley et al. 1975; Hunt 1975; Baldwin 1976; Boote 1976; Barta 1976; Charles-Edwards 1976; Cooper and Thornley 1976; Edwards and Barber 1976; Raper et al. 1978; Hesketh and Jones 1980; Rufty et al. 1981; Reynolds and Thornley 1982.
Shoot activity=carbon uptake rate; root activity=potassium uptake rate
  Hunt and Burnett 1973; Hunt 1975; Cassman et al. 1980; Maynard et al. 1980.
Shoot activity=carbon uptake rate; root activity=water uptake rate
  deWit et al. 1970; Borchert 1973; deWit et al. 1978; van Keulen 1981.
Shoot activity=carbon uptake rate/hormones; root activity=hormone production
  Wilson 1975; Barnes 1979; Richards 1980.

---

the two systems. Davidson (1969) proposed the following quantitative expression of this functional balance between shoots and roots:

$$\text{shoot mass} \times \frac{\text{shoot specific}}{\text{activity}} \; \alpha \; \text{root mass} \times \frac{\text{root specific}}{\text{activity}} \qquad (1)$$

In Table 2.3 are examples of research (both experimental and modeling) which have dealt explicitly with eqn (1). Note that the shoot activity has been studied mainly with respect to the procurement of carbon, whereas root activity has been studied with respect to nitrogen, potassium, water uptake, and hormonal production (Table 2.3).

The shoot:root functional balance model described by eqn (1) has important ecological implications in terms of growth strategies. Partitioning the products of photosynthesis to leaves represents a reinvestment by the plant in its photosynthetic apparatus and hence increases total photosynthesis; concurrently, investment of energy into root growth is necessary for obtaining water and essential nutrients required for growth and photosynthesis. Gadgil and Gadgil (1979) suggest that by maintaining a proper balance between the functions of the root and shoot a plant can maximize its net carbon gain. Furthermore, they state that the root:shoot ratio is not a result of competition between these systems but reflects a balance of functions that ultimately maximizes carbon gain and, hence, success in a given environment. The growth responses and partitioning of root and shoot growth are affected by numerous factors; for example,

sharing of mineral and carbohydrate supplies, species differences, physiological age, aerial environment, defoliation, soil environment and nutritional factors, shared functions of nitrogen metabolism, and growth-
regulator production in roots and shoots (from Boote 1976; also see
Mooney 1972). Figure 2.1 depicts some points of interaction of these
carbon, water, and mineral nutrient processes in the soil-plant (root and
shoot)-atmosphere system.

Partitioning Shoot and Root Growth

The partitioning of growth between shoot and root functions is by far
the major shortcoming in modeling plant growth (Ledig 1976, Thornley
1977). Modelers have attempted to quantify partitioning by using several
general approaches (Hesketh and Jones 1980): (1) setting fixed, time-
invariant empirical partition coefficients for the whole plant; (2) making
organ growth rates a function of substrate availability (for example, carbon
and nitrogen) by utilizing empirical rate coefficients; (3) making organ
growth rates a function of mineral or nutrient uptake using set dryweight
concentrations as thresholds, for example, % nitrogen; (4) basing organ
growth on morphological potential (fixed developmental rates with spec-
ified upper bounds); and (5) using empirical time-variant "priority" allocation schemes (for example, reproductive growth priority over vegetative).
Many models utilize a combination of these approaches reflecting the
availability of data and objectives. For example, Thornley (1972a, b)
developed a transport-resistance based model which partitioned growth
between shoot and root by balancing carbohydrate synthesis in the shoot
with nitrogen uptake by the root (in terms of the transport and utilization of
these two substrates); this model was applied with some success (Cooper
and Thornley 1976) but has been criticized because of its complexity (Fick
et al. 1975, Wareing and Patrick 1975, Ledig 1976). Meyer et al. (1979)
modeled partitioning for soybeans as a closed-loop system based on a
carbon (C)-nitrogen (N) balance between organs. If the N/dry-matter
concentration in tissue dropped below certain designated values for an
organ, its growth rate (hence the C demand) was modified accordingly; a
feedback was obtained by the N-fixation system being C limited. Other
models have partitioned dry matter by descriptive allocation patterns
where net assimilate was partitioned to different organs based on set
percentages or fractions depending upon plant phenology (Curry et al.
1975, Wilkerson et al. 1981). These latter two models and those of Mousi
and Murata (1970), Promnitz (1975), Vanderlip and Arkin (1977), Troughton
(1977), and Wann and Raper (1979) all utilized empirical allometric rela-

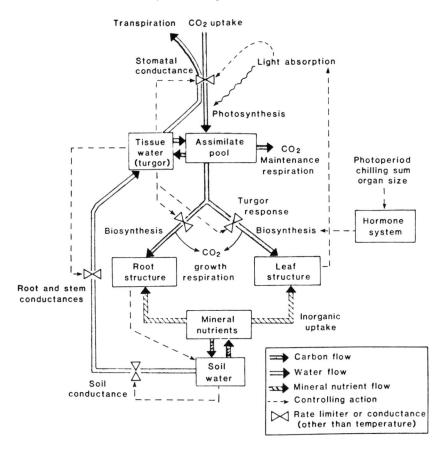

Figure 2.1 Whole-plant interactions between the processes of procurement, translocation, and utilization of water, carbon, and nitrogen. The balance between the shoot and root activities has a significant influence on the magnitude and direction of these fluxes. From Farnum, P., R. Timmis, and J. L. Kulp, Science 219:694–702, © American Association for the Advancement of Science, Washington, D.C., 1983.

tionships for organ dryweight changes, as was the case in our early models of *Larrea* (Cunningham and Reynolds 1978, Reynolds et al. 1980).

Brouwer and deWit (1969) developed a partitioning function that established a balance between shoot and root activities in the sense of eqn (1). They linked the growth rate of shoots and roots to a functional balance or equilibrium between photosynthesis and transpiration (by the shoot) to water and nutrient uptake (by the roots); the partitioning of photosynthate was switched in favor of either the shoot or root depending upon the relative water content of the plant. Their approach, while appealing, lacks a sound phenomenology (Thornley 1976). Fick et al. (1975) adopted a similar strategy for partitioning in their sugar beet model as did Borchert (1973) for a tropical tree growth model.

Reynolds and Thornley's Partitioning Function

Reynolds and Thornley (1982) developed a partitioning model which attempted a compromise between a complex mechanistic approach and a simple, highly empirical approach. This model was structured to examine the interrelationships between the specific growth rate of a plant, its shoot:root ratio, and the shoot and root specific activities [see eqn (1)] which depend directly upon the environment. An interesting feature of this model is the definition of a partitioning function that allows for an adaptive response by a plant to changes in its shoot or root environment via the relative substrate levels within the plant. The partitioning function is briefly described below.

Total dry weight of the plant can be divided into two fractions: structure (W), composed of shoot (W_{sh}) and root (W_r) biomass, that is,

$$W = W_{sh} + W_r \tag{2}$$

and storage, composed of carbon (S_c) and nitrogen (S_n) substrates. By differentiating eqn (2) we get:

$$\frac{dW}{dt} = \frac{dW_{sh}}{dt} + \frac{dW_r}{dt} \tag{3}$$

Partitioning coefficients (λ's) are defined to distribute new growth between shoots and roots so that eqn (3) can be written as

$$\frac{dW}{dt} = \lambda_{sh} \frac{dW}{dt} + \lambda_r \frac{dW}{dt} \tag{4}$$

where $\lambda_{sh} + \lambda_r = 1$. From eqns (3–4) it follows that

$$\lambda_{sh} = \frac{dW_{sh}}{dW} \text{ and } \lambda_r = \frac{dW_r}{dW} \tag{5}$$

and, hence,

$$\frac{\lambda_{sh}}{\lambda_r} = \frac{dW_{sh}}{dW_r} \tag{6}$$

Reynolds and Thornley defined a partitioning function P, the relative rate of specific shoot growth to specific root growth, in terms of the carbon to nitrogen ratio in the storage pools:

$$P = \frac{dW_{sh}/W_{sh}}{dW_r/W_r} = \left[\frac{N/\eta_n}{C/\eta_c} \right]^q \tag{7}$$

where N and C are the whole-plant concentrations (that is, S_n/W and S_c/W) of the nitrogen and carbon substrates, respectively, and η_n, η_c and q are model parameters; the partitioning function is shown graphically in Figure 2.2, with a brief explanation of the parameters. From eqns (5–7) the partitioning coefficients λ_{sh} and λ_r can be derived explicitly as functions of shoot and root dryweights, carbon and nitrogen concentrations, and the parameters η_c, η_n and q:

$$\lambda_{sh} = W_{sh} (N/\eta_n)^q / W_{sh} (N/\eta_n)^q + W_r (C + \eta_c)^q \tag{8a}$$

and

$$\lambda_r = W_r (C/\eta_c)^q / W_{sh} (N/\eta_n)^q + W_r (C + \eta_c)^q \tag{8b}$$

Partitioning between the shoots and roots, then, depends upon the carbon:nitrogen ratio in the storage pools and the extent to which this ratio departs from a reference value given by η_c/η_n (see Figure 2.2); a feedback between shoots and roots is achieved, and in the complete model given in Reynolds and Thornley (1982), the relationship to eqn (1) can be obtained.

SHOOT-ROOT ACTIVITIES IN *LARREA*

Carbon-Nitrogen Balance

—the over-riding importance of water in desert ecosystems means that the cycling of organic materials and nutrients is rarely limiting for primary and secondary production.—Noy-Meir (1973)

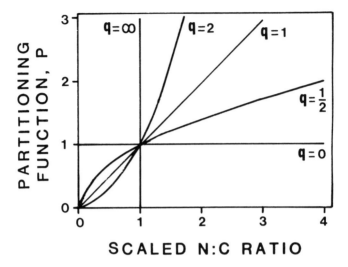

Figure 2.2 Partitioning function P = $(dW_{sh}/W_{sh})/$
(dW_r/W_r) plotted against the scaled nitrogen:carbon ratio
$(N/\eta_n)/(C/\eta_c)$ for various values of q (see eqn 7). Parameter q determines the degree of control that a plant may
exhibit over partitioning, that is, if q = 0 (no control), if q
> 0 (partitioning controlled by levels of N and C as
illustrated), and if q → ∞ (partitioning threshold controlled by levels of N and C). The S:R partitioning depends
upon the reference value η_n/η_c; for example, if N/C >
η_n/η_c then P > 1, that is, $dW_{sh}/W_{sh} > dW_r/W_r$.

In our previous work with *Larrea* we attempted to provide a synthesis
of its physiological ecology in terms of a mathematical model of carbon
allocation. This work emphasized aboveground productivity and the role
of water in controlling the vegetative and reproductive growth. Since
primary productivity in desert ecosystems is generally thought of as being
primarily water limited (Noy-Meir 1973, Evanari et al. 1976, Fisher and
Turner 1978, Ludwig and Whitford 1981) this emphasis seemed justified;
(1) the growth model was developed without a nutrient submodel (see
Cunningham and Reynolds 1978, p. 37), and (2) our validation study
focused on the timing of soil moisture availability (Reynolds and Cunningham 1981). However, in recent years ecologists have recognized the

potential importance of mineral nutrients (particularly nitrogen) as regulators of desert plant productivity (see review by West [1981]).

The role of nitrogen (N) as a limiting factor to plant growth in desert ecosystems has been the subject of numerous recent studies; for example, Mott and McComb (1974) [the Australian desert], Halverson and Patten (1975) [Sonoran Desert], Williams and Bell (1981) [Mojave Desert], and Parker et al. (1982a) [Chihuahuan Desert]. Van Keulen (1981) reported that N, rather than water, may be the most frequent limiting factor in semiarid Mediterranean-type climates. Three recent studies conducted in the Chihuahuan Desert suggest that N may be limiting primary productivity of *Larrea.*

Ettershank et al. (1978) were the first to hypothesize that nitrogen is limiting plant growth in the Chihuahuan Desert, based on their observations of the growth responses of *Larrea* and a perennial grass (*Erioneuron pulchellum*) to N fertilizer. They applied two levels of N fertilizer and concluded that, at the lower rate of N application (25 kg/ha), the shallow-rooted grass (and probably the soil microflora) extracted all available N since grass production was stimulated whereas *Larrea* aboveground production was unaffected. The higher rate of application of N (100 kg/ha) stimulated growth of both species.

Cunningham et al. (1979) examined the effects of season and soil moisture availability on the timing and extent of reproductive and aboveground vegetative growth in *Larrea* plants that received supplemental soil moisture at various times of the year. These data were used to evaluate the *Larrea* growth model (Reynolds and Cunningham 1981). This validation revealed that the model varied in the range of soil moisture conditions over which it was adequate and that when soil moisture remained high for extended periods the model was least adequate. It predicted too much biomass production. We hypothesized that a nutrient deficiency (probably nitrogen) was limiting growth of plants that experienced high soil moisture during the previous growing season. This could have resulted from (1) an increased leaching of nutrients from the soil by the irrigation water, (2) a tie-up of nutrients in new biomass produced under the favorable moisture conditions during the preceding growing seasons, and/or (3) a sequestering of nutrients by soil microorganisms. Similar results have been reported by several Australian researchers who found that plant productivity declined in wet years when preceded by wetter than average years (Trumble and Woodroffe 1954, Charley and Cowling 1968).

Parker et al. (1982b), in a study of carbon and nitrogen dynamics during the decomposition of aboveground litter and roots of the ephemeral pepperweed (*Lepidium lasiocarpum*), proposed a possible mechanism by

James F. Reynolds

Table 2.4. Computation of the growth yield factors (g DW g glucose^{-1}) for *Larrea* shoots (γ_{sh}) and roots (γ_{sh}) based on the chemical composition of leaves and roots, respectively. Data from Oechel et al. (1972), Barbour et al. (1977a) and Rhoades (1977). Approach follows Penning de Vries et al. (1974) and Chung and Barnes (1977).

Compound	Composition (g gDW^{-1})		Production Value[1]	Growth Cost (g glucose)	
	Leaves	Roots		Leaves	Roots
Nitrogen	0.025	0.025	1.58	0.040	0.040
Carbohydrates	0.435	0.700	1.18	0.513	0.826
Lipids	0.040	0.010	3.02	0.121	0.030
Lignin	0.200	0.200	1.90	0.380	0.380
Organic Acids	0.050	0.050	1.48	0.074	0.074
Phenolics	0.250	0.015	1.91	0.478	0.029
Totals	1.00	1.00		1.61	1.376
			$\gamma_{sh} =$	0.62	$\gamma_r = 0.727$

[1]Biosynthetic efficiencies (g glucose used to produce 1 g biomass).

which N availability to *Larrea* may be, in part, a function of ephemeral plant production. This study was conducted in the Chihuahuan Desert, near the Ettershank et al. (1978) and Reynolds and Cunningham (1981) study sites. Briefly, their hypothesis is as follows: Adequate fall and winter moisture will result in an abundance of spring ephemerals which utilize N made available by high mineralization rates resulting from the moist soils. Before summer rains the spring ephemerals die, tying up N in organic litter; N-mineralization is very slow during this dry period. Summer rains stimulate decomposition of the abundant ephemeral plant litter resulting in increased decomposer biomass (mainly fungi). The fungi develop a network of hyphae around the decomposing ephemeral roots which acts as a sieve, removing mineralized nutrients from the downward moving water column. Hence, N is sequestered by the fungi and is unavailable for the deeper rooted *Larrea* shrubs. Parker et al. cite circumstantial evidence presented by Ludwig and Flavill (1979) which shows maximum *Larrea* production during wet summers that follow a dry fall and winter (and, apparently, a low spring annual plant production).

The above studies suggest that N is possibly limiting *Larrea* primary productivity in the Chihuahuan Desert. However, none examined belowground productivity. Without knowledge of belowground dynamics, it's difficult to say whether a real decrease in production or simply a shift in the shoot:root allocation pattern accounts for the observed results. A clearer understanding of the actual growth dynamics of *Larrea* in response to moisture and nutrient availability will be required before the importance of this species to other ecosystem processes—for example, nutrient cycling, water flux, and energy flow—can be fully evaluated. Our current knowledge of *Larrea* growth dynamics are consistent with eqn (1), at least in terms of the integrative nature of plant growth. I believe that one key to understanding the dynamic aspects of the growth strategy for creosotebush lies in modeling the functional balance between aboveground and belowground processes. This is not to suggest that the proportionality in eqn (1) is necessarily constant but, instead, that a dynamic functional balance exists which reflects both current and past environmental conditions. A cost-income analysis model can be used to evaluate the outcomes of various functional balance strategies and to assess which strategies might provide viable options for success in desert environments. These viable strategies then become experimentally falsifiable hypotheses relative to the physiological adaptations of the species.

Cost-Income Analysis

The partitioning coefficients in eqn (8) can be used to compute the total carbon (energy) costs for constructing and maintaining roots (fine and suberized) and shoots (leaves and stems) over a fixed period of time:

$$\text{Root costs} = \int_0^t \{(1-\tau)\, \gamma_r^{-1}\, \lambda_r\, (dW/dt) + \Theta A W_r + M_r\, W_r\}\, dt \quad (9a)$$

$$\text{Shoot costs} = \int_0^t \{(\gamma_{sh}^{-1} + \alpha\, f_n)\, \lambda_{sh}\, (dW/dt) + M_{sh}\, W_{sh}\}\, dt \quad (9b)$$

where

τ = C translocation costs (g CH_2O/g CH_2O)
α = N translocation costs (g CH_2O/g N)
Θ = N uptake costs (g CH_2O/g N)
f_n = fractional nitrogen content of dry matter (g N/g DW)
γ_r, γ_{sh} = growth yield for roots (r) and shoots (sh) (g DW/g CH_2O substrate)
A = unit absorption rate for roots (mol N/g DW/unit time)
M_r, M_{sh} = maintenance respiration (g CH_2O/g DW/unit time)
λ_r, λ_{sh} = partitioning coefficients (eqns 8a–8b)

As can be seen from eqn (9), the total energy costs are broken down into construction (the growth yield factor), translocation, uptake, and maintenance (see Penning de Vries et al. 1974, Thornley 1976, de Wit et al. 1978, Miller and Stoner 1979).

The biomass construction costs of different plant parts are based on Penning de Vries's (1974) determination of the growth yield resulting from different biochemical pathways of synthesis. From eqn (9) the rate at which the carbon substrate is utilized for total plant growth is

$$\gamma^{-1} \frac{dW}{dt} \tag{10}$$

where the growth yield can be partitioned into shoot and root yield by

$$\gamma^{-1} = \lambda_{sh}\, \gamma_{sh}^{-1} + \lambda_r\, \gamma_r^{-1} \tag{11}$$

Growth respiration is therefore obtained from:

$$\frac{(1-\gamma)}{\gamma} \cdot \frac{dW}{dt} = \left\{ \lambda_{sh} \frac{(1-\gamma_{sh})}{\gamma_{sh}} + \lambda_r \frac{(1-\gamma_r)}{\gamma_r} \right\} \frac{dW}{dt} \tag{12}$$

Utilizing data on the biochemical composition of *Larrea* leaves and roots given in Oechel et al. (1972), Barbour et al. (1977b), and Rhoades (1977), I computed values of γ_{sh} and γ_r to be, respectively, 0.621 and 0.727 (see Table 2.4). The higher costs for shoots can be seen to be related to the higher percentage of composition of phenolics and lipids, both energetically expensive to synthesize (Table 2.4). It's clear from this that variations in the chemistry of plant parts (leaves, flowers, fruits, seeds, stems, roots, and other parts) are important in assessing the relative costs of shoot versus root growth (Mooney and Gulmon 1979, 1982; Miller 1979, Miller and Stoner 1979).

To illustrate one facet of the adaptive strategy of *Larrea*—the shoot-to-root ratio of our simulation model (Reynolds et al. 1980) was modified to include the Reynolds and Thornley (1982) partitioning function (see eqns 7–8) and ran for t = 30 days. For ease of interpretation, the environmental driving variables (irradiance, soil moisture, air and soil temperatures, and so forth) were fixed to obtain constant shoot and root activities (eqn 1) and only vegetative growth was considered. Soil moisture was set to give maximum photosynthesis rates based on the model in Reynolds et al. (1979). The growth rate of structure was assumed to be a function of carbon and nitrogen substrate concentrations:

$$\frac{dW}{dt} = kCNW \qquad (13)$$

where k is a growth rate parameter. The *Larrea* model was then executed using various partitioning strategies (achieved by varying the C:N ratio in the storage pools—see eqn 7). For each simulation the following were determined: the average relative growth rate, that is,

$$\overline{RGR} = \frac{1}{t-t_0} \int_{t_0}^{t} \left\{ \frac{1}{W} \cdot \frac{dW}{dt} \right\} dt, \qquad (14)$$

total carbon and nitrogen gain (input), total shoot and root costs (eqn 9), and shoot to root (S:R) ratios. The results are shown in Figure 2.3, which depicts the various trade-offs and feedbacks between the root (supplying N and water) and the shoot (supplying C).

As expected, an increase in the S:R ratio resulted in an increase in the absolute size of the shoot system and, hence, total C input (Figure 2.3). The largest root system, however, unexpectedly occurred at a S:R ratio of 0.75; further decreases in the S:R ratio below this level (under the specific conditions of the simulation) apparently resulted in C-limited growth and, therefore, a decrease in both root and shoot biomass (Figure 2.3). The average relative growth rate ($\overline{RGR}$) was maximum at a S:R ratio of 1.27. The maximum $\overline{RGR}$ corresponded to a ratio of 1.6 for the total shoot costs to root costs (eqn 9) (Figure 2.3).

Growth Strategy Implications

Stress-tolerant species, particularly desert perennials, are usually characterized as possessing low S:R ratios (see reviews by Chapin 1980 and Barbour 1973, 1981). Since these species have low capacities for photosynthesis (discussed earlier) and nutrient absorption (Chapin 1980), a simple strategy to increase both water and nutrient acquisition would be to increase total root biomass. Chapin (1980) argues that high nutrient absorptivities of roots per se would offer little advantage to species in infertile soils, given that absorption is mainly limited by diffusion from the bulk soil to the roots. While this argument has validity, there appears to be little evidence (although more data are needed) that desert perennials necessarily have low S:R ratios (Barbour 1973, 1981; Ludwig 1977).

I have summarized some reported S:R ratios for field studies of *Larrea* in Table 2.5. A great deal of variation in this ratio exists, related to age, to

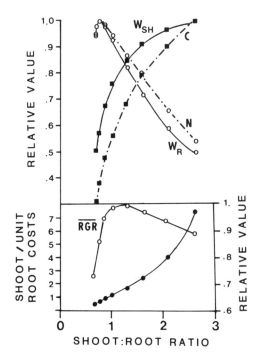

Figure 2.3 Results of *Larrea* simulation model. Illustrated are the effects of various shoot:root partitioning schemes on the sizes of the shoot (W_{sh}), and root (W_r), total carbon (C) and nitrogen (N) uptake over the thirty-day simulation, the average daily relative growth rate ($\overline{RGR}$, eqn 14), and the total shoot costs per unit root cost (•) (eqn 9b/eqn 9a). W_{sh}, W_r, C, N, and $\overline{RGR}$ are all expressed as relative values.

location, and between studies. Of course, if the S:R ratio represents a dynamic index which varies according to the overall balance of growth it's not surprising to see the wide diversity of reported values. Orians and Solbrig (1977) state that "the difference between a (S:R) ratio that maximizes benefit in terms of both leaf and root costs and income and the (S:R) ratio that supplies the maximal amount of water under all circumstances can be considerable." This is supported by the results shown in Figure 2.3 for *Larrea*.

Table 2.5. Some reported shoot:root ratios for *L. tridentata*. Expanded from Barbour (1973).

Location	Age (years)	S:R Ratio	Range	Reference
Arizona	1	2.00		Chew and Chew (1965)
	3	3.00		
	5	2.75		
	15	3.42		
	25	4.50		
	35	3.92		
	45	2.77		
	55	2.65		
	65	2.37		
SW USA	0.11	1.67		Barbour (1973)
Nevada	0.16	2.56		Wallace et al. (1970)
	?	———	0.66–1.04	Wallace and Rommey (1972)
	?	0.40	0.33–0.63	Wallace et al. (1980a)
	?	1.42		Wallace et al. (1980b)
	?	3.00		Wallace et al. (1980c)
	Mature	0.93		Bamberg et al. (1973)
New Mexico	Mature	0.42	0.15–1.56	Singh (1964)
	Mature	1.84		Ludwig et al. (1975)
	Mature	1.11	0.37–4.35	Ludwig (1977)
California	Mature	4.00		Garcia-Moya and McKell (1970)

Maximum root biomass occurred at a S:R ratio of 0.75 (Figure 2.3); at this ratio total N input, computed on a root dry weight basis (see parameter A, eqn [9a]), was maximal whereas total C input and the RGR were about 38% and 86%, respectively, of maximum observed values. A small increase in the S:R ratio from 0.75 to 0.87 decreased total N input only slightly, yet total C input increased to ca. 47% of maximum while the RGR increased from 86% to 95% of maximum. In fact, a S:R ratio anywhere in the range from approximately 0.8 to 2.5 can be seen to result in 90 to 100% of the maximum RGR under the conditions of this simulation (Figure 2.3). Thus, the partitioning of biomass between shoot and root functions in *Larrea* may possibly vary substantially during vegetative growth with only a relatively slight effect on the overall growth rate. Under conditions of low moisture or nutrient availability, a lower S:R ratio might be advantageous to ensure adequate supply of these limited resources. However, increases in the S:R ratio would be advantageous for maximizing total C input and, although the total growth rate of the plant may be N limited, the decline in RGR is a relatively slowly decreasing function compared to C limitation (Figure 2.3). This interpretation of Figure 2.3 for *Larrea* is supported by numerous observations of stress-tolerant plants (see Grime 1977, 1979; Orians and Solbrig 1977, Chapin 1980, Gutschick 1981). For example, Chapin (1980) proposes that species with inherently low growth rates will, nevertheless, be functioning closer to their optimal growth under stress conditions than plants with higher growth rates under similar stresses.

CONCLUDING REMARKS

Whatever the worth of the empirical evidence that plants tend to optimize . . . , the theory is of limited conceptual value if it is without a plausible explanation as to why plants are so adapted.— Cowan (1982)

Many aspects of the resource allocation strategies of *Larrea* are of interest to desert ecologists. The modeling approach that I have presented in this paper may be a helpful tool for addressing some of these problems; each can be expressed in precise mathematical terms and in varying degrees of physiological detail depending upon specific objectives. For example, is there a S:R ratio that maximizes both C and N income in a given environment? Various aspects of the total physiology of the plant must be integrated to examine this, for example, vegetative and reproductive growth, root area:leaf area relationship, long-term versus short-term investment returns (leaves versus roots), and so forth. Is there a given point for the switch from vegetative to reproductive growth that will maximize seed production? Associated with this are questions concerning the optimal use of N—that is, the amount of seed produced per unit N available (Fisher 1981).

Does the seasonal change in % N content of plant parts have a significant impact on the balance between shoot and root activities? Freeman (1982) has demonstrated that the total leaf N content varies seasonally in *Larrea*. Mooney and Gulmon (1979, 1982), Miller (1979), Miller and Stoner (1979), and Field (1983) have discussed the potential importance of such N variations in the overall growth processes of plants, particularly for C procurement. In terms of the balance between C income and N uptake, and % N content, various partitioning strategies can be examined. Richards et al. (1979) experimentally tested Davidson's functional equilibrium hypothesis (see eqn [1]) for reproductively growing plants; the presence of fruit represented an important sink for C and N which resulted in a redistribution of growth and N content of individual organs. The specific activities of the shoot and root accompanying these changes maintained a balance between shoot and root functions. These types of data, as yet, do not exist for *Larrea*.

As mentioned earlier, the lack of information on the dynamics of belowground productivity for *Larrea* is one of the major gaps in our knowledge of this species. Such information is indispensable for developing a dynamic model of its adaptive strategy. For example, what is the impact of root turnover rates (both fine and suberized roots) on providing the plant with N and water at minimal costs, given some environmental regime and shoot activity? Caldwell (1976, 1979) and Fowkes and Landsberg (1981) discuss some evolutionary considerations involved in the minimization of costs associated with root systems; in an adaptive strategy model the total balance of growth (above and belowground) must be considered simultaneously.

What is the magnitude of energy allocation to protection (herbivory) functions, for example, phenolic compounds in the leaf, in terms of affecting the shoot:root balance? Mooney and Chu (1974), McLaughlin and Shriner (1980), Mattson (1980), and Mooney and Gulmon (1982) emphasize the importance of such energy allocation in plants. As these compounds are expensive to produce, it would be of interest to simulate various patterns of phenolic production and leaf longevity in relation to seasonal growth. Seasonal changes in such costs can be incorporated in the growth yield coefficient, γ_{sh}.

Does *Larrea* exhibit "optimal" growth strategies? Or is the plant in some sort of dynamic equilibrium, reflecting a multitude of trade-offs for its limited resources? Obviously, there are numerous problems to overcome in clarifying the enigmatic facets of its ecology. It will be necessary to combine an understanding of its life history, morphology, and physiology to achieve a theoretical framework for developing a model of its adaptative strategy. Thornley (1977), commenting on the integration of plant activities at the whole-plant level, stresses the importance of quantifying the empirical evidence accumulated by researchers on root:shoot interactions and dry-matter partitioning. Jones (1980) and Loomis et al. (1979) recommend the use of models as tools to integrate our knowledge of partitioning in plants because of the many interacting factors governing this process and the significance of identifying "certain optimal hypothesis" of partitioning. Geiger (1979) states that an analysis of the control systems governing partitioning promises to provide insights into various plant processes. I am optimistic that the modeling approach discussed in this paper will be a helpful tool in our efforts to develop a better understanding of the ecology of the creosotebush, as well as other desert species.

ACKNOWLEDGMENTS

I wish to express my gratitude to Gary Cunningham for his critical review of this paper and his tireless (and ongoing) efforts to educate me about the ecology of *Larrea*. Thanks are also due to Tom Wentworth for helpful suggestions.

REFERENCES

Baldwin, J. P. 1976. Competition for plant nutrients in soil: a theoretical approach. Journal of Agricultural Science (Cambridge) 87:341–356.

Barbour, M. G. 1969. Age and space distribution of the desert shrub *Larrea divaricata*. Ecology 50:679–685.

Barbour, M. G. 1973. Desert dogma reexamined: root/shoot productivity and plant spacing. American Midland Naturalist 89:41–57.

Barbour, M. G., J. A. MacMahon, S. A. Bamberg, and J. A. Ludwig. 1977a. The structure and distribution of *Larrea* communities, pp. 48–91. *In:* T. J. Mabry, J. H. Hunziker, and D. R. Difeo (eds.). Creosote bush. Biology and chemistry of *Larrea* in new world deserts. Dowden, Hutchinson, and Ross; Stroudsburg, Pennsylvania.

Barbour, M. G., G. L. Cunningham, W. C. Oechel and S. A. Bamberg. 1977b. Growth and development, form and function, pp. 48–91. *In:* T. J. Mabry, J. H. Hunziker, and D. R. Difeo (eds.). Creosote bush. Biology and chemistry of *Larrea* in new world deserts. Dowden, Hutchinson, Ross; Stroudsburg, Pennsylvania.

Barbour, M. G. 1981. Plant-plant interactions, pp. 33–49. *In:* D. W. Goodall and R. A. Perry (eds.). Arid land ecosystems: Structure, functioning and management, vol. 2, Cambridge University Press.

Barnes, A. 1979. Vegetable plant part relationships. IV. An interpretation of growth regulator experiments with root crops. Annals of Botany 43:513–522.

Barta, A. 1976. Transport and distribution of CO_2 assimilate in *Lolium perenne* in response to varying nitrogen supply to halves of a divided root system. Plant Physiology 38:48–52.

Boote, K. J. 1976. Root-shoot relationships. Soil Crop Science, Florida 36:15–23.

Borchert, R. 1973. Simulation of rhythmic tree growth under constant conditions. Physiologcia Plantarum 29:173–180.

Brouwer, R., and C. T. deWit. 1968. A similation model of plant growth with special attention to root growth and its consequences, pp. 224–242. Proceedings of the 15th Easter School of Agricultural Science. University of Nottingham.

Burk, J. H., and W. A. Dick-Peddie. 1973. Comparative production of *Larrea divaricata* Cav. on three geomorphic surfaces in southern New Mexico. Ecology 54:1094–1102.

Caldwell, M. M. 1976. Root extension and water absorption, pp. 64–85. *In:* O. L. Lange, L. Kapen, and E. E. Schulze (eds.). Water and Plant Life, Springer-Verlag, New York.

Caldwell, M. M. 1979. Root structure: the considerable cost of belowground function, pp. 408–427. *In:* O. T. Solbrig, S. Jain, G. B. Johnson, and P. H. Raven (eds.). Topics in plant population biology, Columbia University Press, New York.

Campos-Lopez, C., T. J. Mabry, and S. Fernandez-Tavizon (eds.). 1979. *Larrea*. Centro de Investigacion en Quimicia Aplicada, Saltillo, Mexico.

Cassman, K. G., A. S. Whitney, and K. P. Stockinger. 1980. Root growth and dry matter distribution of soybean as affected by phosphorus stress, nodulation, and nitrogen source. Crop Science 20:239–242.

Chapin, F. S. 1980. The mineral nutrition of wild plants. Annual Review of Ecological Systematics 21:233–260.

Charley, J. L., and S. W. Cowling. 1968. Changes in soil nutrient status resulting from overgrazing and their consequences in plant communities of semi-arid zones. Proceedings of the Ecological Society of Australia 3:28–38.

Charles-Edwards, D. 1976. Shoot and root activities during steady-state plant growth. Annals of Botany 40:767–772.

Chew, R. M., and A. E. Chew. 1976. The primary productivity of a desert shrub (*Larrea tridentata*) community. Ecological Monographs 35:355–375.

Chung, H. H., and R. L. Barnes. 1977. Photosynthate allocation in *Pinus taeda*. I. Substrate requirement for synthesis of shoot biomass. Canadian Journal of Forest Research 7:106–111.

Cody, M. L. 1974. Optimization in ecology. Science 183:1156–1164.

Cohen, D. 1968. A general model of optimal reproduction in a randomly varying environment. Journal of Ecology 56:219–228.

Cohen, D. 1971. Maximizing final yield when growth is limited by time or by limiting resources. Journal of Theoretical Biology 33:299–307.

Cooper, A. J., and A. H. M. Thornley. 1976. Response of dry matter partitioning, growth, and carbon and nitrogen levels in the tomato plant to changes in root temperature: experiment and theory. Annals of Botany 40:1139–1152.

Cowan, I. R., and G. D. Farquhar. 1977. Stomatal function in relation to leaf metabolism and environment. Symposium of the Society of Experimental Biology 31:471–505.

Cowan, I. R. 1982. Regulation of water use in relation to carbon gain in higher plants, pp. 589–614. *In:* O. L. Lang, P. S. Nobel, C. B. Osmond, and H. Ziegler (eds.). Physiological plant ecology II, Water relations and carbon assimilation, Springer-Verlag, Berlin.

Cunningham, G. L., and J. F. Reynolds. 1978. A similation model of primary production and carbon allocation in the creosotebush (*Larrea tridentata* [DC] Cov.). Ecology 58:37–52.

Cunningham, G. L., J. P. Syvertsen, J. F. Reynolds, and J. M. Willson. 1979. Some effects of soil-moisture availability on above-ground production and reproductive allocation in *Larrea tridentata* (DC) Cov. Oecologia 40:113–123.

Curry, R. B., C. H. Baker, and J. G. Streeter. 1975. SOYMOD I: a dynamic simulator of soybean growth and development. Transcripts of the American Society of Agricultural Engineers 18:963–974.

Davidson, R. L. 1969. Effect of root/leaf temperature differentials on root/shoot ratios in some pasture grasses and clover. Annals of Botany 33:561–569.

Denholm, J. V. 1975. Necessary condition for maximizing yield in a senescing two-phase plant. Journal of Theoretical Biology 52:251–254.

de Wit, C. T., R. Brouwer, and F. W. T. Penning deVries. 1970. The simulation of photosynthetic systems, pp. 47–50. *In:* I. Setlik (ed.). Prediction and measurement of photosynthetic productivity. Proceedings of the IBP/PP Technical meeting. Trebon, Pudoc, Wageningen.

de Wit, C. T. et al. 1978. Simulation of assimilation, respiration and transpiration of crops. Simulation Monographs, Pudoc, Wageningen.

Edwards, J. H., and S. A. Barber. 1976. Nitrogen flux into corn roots as influenced by shoot requirements. Agronomy Journal 689:471–473.

Ettershank, G., J. Ettershank, M. Bryant, and W. G. Whitford. 1978. Effects of nitrogen
   fertilization on primary production in a Chihuahuan Desert ecosystem. Journal of Arid
   Environments 1:135–139.
Evenari, M., S. Bamberg, D. D. Schulze, L. Kappen, O. L. Lange, and W. Buschbom.
   1976. The biomass production of some higher plants in Near-Eastern and American
   deserts, pp. 121–127. In: J. P. Cooper (ed.). Photosynthesis and productivity in dif-
   ferent environments, Cambridge University Press, London.
Fick, G. W., R. W. Loomis, and W. A. Williams. 1975. Sugar beet, pp. 259–295. In: L. T.
   Evans (ed.). Crop Physiology, Cambridge University Press, London.
Field, C. 1983. Allocating leaf nitrogen for the maximization of carbon gain: leaf age as a
   control on the allocation program. Oecologia 56:341–347.
Fisher, R. A., and N. C. Turner. 1978. Plant productivity in the arid and semi-arid zones.
   Annual Review of Plant Physiology 29:277–317.
Fisher, R. A. 1981. Optimizing the use of water and nitrogen through breeding of crops.
   Plant and Soil 58:249–271.
Fowkes, N. D., and J. J. Landsberg. 1981. Optimal root systems in terms of water uptake
   and movement, pp. 109–128. In: D. A. Rose, and D. A. Charles-Edwards (eds.).
   Mathematics and plant physiology, Academic Press, New York.
Freeman, C. F. 1982. Seasonal variation in leaf nitrogen in creosotebush (Larrea tridentata
   [D.C.] Cov. Zygophyllaceae). Southwestern Naturalist 27:354–356.
Gadgil, M., and W. H. Bossert. 1970. Life historical consequences of natural selection.
   American Naturalist 104:1–24.
Gadgil, M., and S. Gadgil. 1979. Adaptive significance of the relation between root and
   shoot growth. Journal of the Indian Institute of Science 61:25–40.
Garcia-Moya, E., and C. M. McKell. 1970. Contribution of shrubs to the nitrogen economy
   of a desert wash plant community. Ecology 51:81–88.
Geiger, D. R. 1979. Control of partitioning and export of carbon in leaves of higher plants.
   Botanical Gazette 140:241–248.
Gifford, R. M., and L. T. Evans. 1981. Photosynthesis, carbon partitioning, and yield.
   Annual Review of Plant Physiology 32:485–509.
Givinish, T. 1979. On the adaptive significance of leaf form, pp. 375–407. In: O. T. Solbrig,
   S. Jain, G. B. Johnson, and P. H. Raven (eds.). Topics in plant population biology,
   Columbia University Press, New York.
Grime, J. P. 1977. Evidence for the existence of three primary strategies in plants and its
   relevance to ecological and evolutionary theory. American Naturalist 111:1169–1194.
Grime, J. P. 1979. Plant strategies and vegetation processes. John Wiley and Sons, Chiches-
   ter.
Grime, J. P. 1982. The concept of strategies: use and abuse. Journal of Ecology 70:863–865.
Gulmon, S. L., and C. C. Chu. 1981. The effects of light and nitrogen on photosynthesis,
   leaf characteristics, and dry matter allocation in the chaparral shrub, Diplacus auran-
   tiacus. Oecologia 49:207–212.
Gutschick, V. P. 1981. Evolved strategies in nitrogen acquisition by plants. American
   Naturalist 118:607–637.
Halvorson, W. L., and D. T. Patten. 1975. Productivity and flowering of winter ephemerals
   in relation to Sonoran Desert shrubs. American Midland Naturalist 93:311–319.
Hesketh, J. D., and J. W. Jones. 1980. Integrating traditional growth analysis techniques
   with recent modeling of carbon and nitrogen metabolism. In: J. D. Hesketh, and J. W.
   Jones (eds.). Predicting photosynthesis for ecosystem models, Vol. 1, CRC Press.
Hickman, J. C. 1977. Energy allocation and niche differentiation in four coexisting annual
   species of Polygonum in western North America. Journal of Ecology 65:317–326.

Hubbell, S. P. and P. A. Werner. 1979. On measuring the intrinsic rate of increase of populations with heterogeneous life histories. American Naturalist 113:277–293.

Hunt, R. 1975. Further observations on root-shoot equilibria in perennial ryegrass. Annals of Botany 39:745–755.

Hunt, R., and J. A. Burnett. 1973. The effects of light intensity and external potassium level on root/shoot ratio and rates of potassium uptake in perennial ryegrass (*Lolium perenne* L.). Annals of Botany 37:519–537.

Jones, H. G. 1980. Interactions and integration of adaptive responses to water stress: The implications of an unpredictable environment, pp. 353–365. *In:* N. C. Turner, and P. J. Kramer (eds.). Adaptation of plants to water and high temperatures stress, John Wiley and Sons, New York.

King, D., and J. Roughgarten. 1982a. Graded allocation between vegetative and reproductive growth for annual plants in growing seasons of random length. Theoretical Population Biology 22:1–16.

King, D., and J. Roughgarten. 1982b. Multiple switches between vegetative and reproductive growth in annual plants. Theoretical Population Biology 21:194–204.

King, D., and J. Roughgarten. 1983. Energy allocation patterns of the California grassland annuals *Plantago erecta* and *Clarkia rubicunda.* Ecology 64:16–24.

Layzell, D. B., J. S. Pate, C. A. Atkins, and D. T. Canvin. 1981. Partitioning of carbon and nitrogen and the nutrition of root and shoot apex in a nodulated legume. Plant Physiology 67:30–36.

Ledig, F. T. 1976. Physiological genetics, photosynthesis and growth models, pp. 21–54. *In:* M. G. R. Cannel and F. T. Last (eds.). Tree physiology and yield improvement, Academy Press, New York.

Loomis, R. S., R. Rabbinge, and E. Ng. 1979. Explanatory models in crop physiology. Annual Review of Plant Physiology 30:339–367.

Ludwig, J. A., J. F. Reynolds, and P. D. Whitson. 1975. Size-biomass relationships of several Chihuahuan Desert shrubs. American Midland Naturalist 94:451–461.

Ludwig, J. A. 1977. Distribution adaptations of root systems in desert environments. *In:* J. K. Marshall (ed.). The belowground ecosystem symposium: a synthesis of plant-associated processes, Range Science Department Science Series Number 26, Colorado State University, Fort Collins, Colorado.

Ludwig, J. A., and P. Flavill. 1979. Productivity patterns of *Larrea* in the northern Chihuahuan Desert, pp. 139–150. *In:* E. Campos-Lopez, T. J. Mabry, S. Fernandez-Tavizon (eds.). *Larrea.* Centro de Investigacion en Quimica Aplicada, Saltillo, Mexico.

Ludwig, J. A., and W. G. Whitford. 1981. Short-term water and energy flow in arid ecosystems, pp. 271–299. *In:* D. W. Goodall, and R. A. Perry (eds.). Arid land ecosystems: Structure, functioning and management, Vol. 2, Cambridge University Press.

Mabry, T. J., J. H. Hunziker, and D. R. Difeo (eds.). 1977. Creostote bush. Biology and chemistry of *Larrea* in new world deserts. Dowden, Hutchinson, and Ross; Stroudsburg, Pennsylvania.

Magambo, M. J. S. and M. G. R. Cannell. 1981. Dry matter production and partition in relation to yield of tea. Experimental Agriculture 17:33–38.

Mattson, W. J. 1980. Herbivory in relation to plant nitrogen content. Annual Review of Ecological Systematics 11:119–161.

Maynard, D. N., O. A. Lorenz, and V. Magnifico. 1980. Growth and potassium partitioning in tomatoes. Journal of the American Society of Horticultural Science 105:79–82.

McLaughlin, S. B., and D. S. Shriner. 1980. Allocation of resources to defense and repair, pp. 407–431. *In:* J. G. Horsfall, and E. B. Cowling (eds.). Plant disease, Vol. 5, How plants defend themselves, Academic Press, New York.

Mendelssohn, R. 1976. Optimization problems associated with a Leslie matrix. American Naturalist 110:339–349.

Meyer, G. E., R. B. Curry, J. G. Streeter, and H. J. Mederski. 1979. SOYMOD/OARDC: A dynamic simulator of soybean growth, development and seed yield. Ohio Agricultural Research and Development Center, Research Bulletin 1113.

Miller, P. C., and W. A. Stoner. 1979. Canopy structural and environmental interactions, pp. 428–458. *In:* O. T. Solbrig, S. Jain, G. B. Johnson, and P. H. Raven (eds.). Topics in plant population biology, Columbia University Press, New York.

Miller, P. C. 1979. Quantitative plant ecology, pp. 179–232. *In:* D. J. Horn, G. R. Stairs, and R. D. Mitchell (eds.). Analysis of ecological systems, Ohio State University Press, Columbus, Ohio.

Moldau, H. 1974. Influence of water deficit on plant matter increase. *In:* Izvestija Akad Nauk Estomii, Seres Biologija 23:348–357.

Moldau, H. 1977. Maximization of the plant reproductive yield under water stress, pp. 140–145. *In:* K. Unger (ed.). Biophysikalische Analyse pflanzlicher Systeme, Veb Gustav Fisher Verlag Jena.

Mooney, H. A. 1972. The carbon balance of plants. Annual Review of Ecology and Systematics 3:315–346.

Mooney, H. A., and C. Chu. 1974. Seasonal carbon allocation in *Heteromales arbutifolia*, a California evergreenshrub. Oecologia 14:295–306.

Mooney, H. A., O. Bjorkman, and G. J. Collatz. 1977. Photosynthetic acclimation to temperature and water stress in the desert shrub, *Larrea divaricata*. Carnegie Institute Year Book 76:328–335.

Mooney, H. A., and S. L. Gulmon. 1979. Environmental and evolutionary constraints on the photosynthetic characteristics of higher plants, pp. 316–337. *In:* O. T. Solbrig, S. Jain, G. B. Johnson, and P. H. Raven (eds.). Topics in plant population biology, Columbia University Press, New York.

Mooney, H. A. 1980. Seasonality and gradients in the study of stress adaptation, pp. 279–294. *In:* N. C. Turner, and P. J. Kramer (eds.). Adaptation of plants to water and high temperature stress, Wiley and Sons, New York.

Mooney, H. A., S. L. Gulmon. 1982. Constraints on leaf structure and function in reference to herbivory. BioScience 32:198–206.

Monsi, M., and Y. Murata. 1970. Development of photosynthetic systems as influenced by distribution of matter, pp. 115–129. *In:* I. Setlik (ed.). Prediction and measurements of photosynthetic productivity, Pudoc, Wageningen.

Mott, J. J., and A. J. McComb. 1974. Patterns in annual vegetation and soil microlief in an arid region of western Australia. Journal of Ecology 62:115–126.

Novoa, R., and R. S. Loomis. 1981. Nitrogen and plant production. Plant and Soil 68:177–204.

Noy-Meir, I. 1973. Desert ecosystems: Environment and producers. Annual Review of Ecological Systematics 4:25–51.

Odening, W. R., B. R. Strain, and W. C. Oechel. 1974. The effect of decreasing water potential on net CO_2 exchange of intact desert shrubs. Ecology 55:1086–1095.

Oechel, W. C., B. R. Strain, and W. R. Odening. 1972. Tissue water potential, photosynthesis, ^{14}C-labeled photosynthate utilization, and growth in the desert shrub *Larrea divaricata* Cav. Ecological Monographs 42:127–141.

Orians, G. H. and O. T. Solbrig. 1977. A cost-income model of leaves and roots with special reference to arid and semiarid areas. American Naturalist 111:677–689.

Paltridge, G. W., and J. V. Denholm. 1974. Plant yield and the switch from vegetative to reproductive growth. Journal of Theoretical Biology 44:23–34.

Parker, L. W., H. G. Fowler, G. Ettershank, and W. G. Whitford. 1982. The effects of subterranean termite removal on desert soil nitrogen and ephemeral flora. Journal of Arid Environments 5:53–59.

Parker, L. W., P. F. Santos, J. Phillips, and W. G. Whitford. 1984. Carbon and nitrogen dynamics during the decomposition of litter and roots of a Chihuahuan Desert annual. Ecological Monographs 54:339–360.

Parkhurst, D., and O. Loucks. 1972. Optimal leaf size in relation to environment. Journal of Ecology 60:505–537.

Penning de Vries, F. W. T., A. H. M. Brunsting, and H. H. Van Laar. 1974. Products, requirements, and efficiency of biosynthesis: A quantitative approach. Journal of Theoretical Biology 45:399–377.

Promnitz, L. C. 1975. A photosynthate allocation model for tree growth. Photosynthetica 9:1–15.

Raper, C. D., D. L. Osmond, M. Wann, and W. W. Weeks. 1978. Interdependence of root and shoot activities in determining nitrogen uptake rate of roots. Botanical Gazette 130:289–294.

Reynolds, J. F., G. L. Cunningham and J. P. Syvertsen. 1979. A net CO_2 exchange model for *Larrea tridentata*. Photosynthetica 13:279–286.

Reynolds, J. F., B. R. Strain, G. L. Cunningham, and K. R. Knoerr. 1980. Predicting primary productivity for forest and desert ecosystem models, pp. 169–207. *In:* J. D. Hesketh, and J. W. Jones (eds.). Predicting photosynthesis for ecosystem models, Vol. II, CRC Press, Boca Raton, Florida.

Reynolds, J. F., and G. L. Cunningham. 1981. Validation of a primary productivity model of the desert shrub *Larrea tridentata* using soil moisture augmentation experiments. Oecologia 51:357–363.

Reynolds, J. F., and J. H. M. Thornley. 1982. A shoot:root partitioning model. Annals of Botany 49:585–597.

Rhoades, D. F. 1977. The antiherbivore chemistry of *Larrea*, pp. 135–175. *In:* T. J. Mabry, J. H. Hunziker, and D. R. DiFeo, Jr. (eds.). Creosotebush: biology and chemistry of *Larrea* in new world deserts, US/IBP Synthesis Series, Dowden, Hutchinson, and Ross; Stroudsburg, Pennsylvania.

Richards, D., F. H. Goubran, and K. E. Collins. 1979. Root-shoot equilibria in fruiting tomato plants. Annals of Botany 43:401–404.

Richards, D. 1980. Root-shoot interactions: effects of cytokinin applied to the root and/or shoot of apple seedlings. Scientia Horticulturia 12:143–152.

Rufty, T. W., C. D. Raper and W. A. Jackson. 1981. N assimilation, root growth and whole plant response of soybean to root temperature and to carbon dioxide and light in the aerial environment. New Phytologist 88:607–619.

Russell, R. S. 1977. Plant root systems. McGraw-Hill, London.

Schaffer, W. M., and M. D. Gadgil. 1975. Selection for optimal life histories in plants, pp. 142–157. *In:* M. L. Cody, and J. M. Diamond (eds.). Ecology and evolution of communities, Harvard University Press, Cambridge.

Singh, S. P. 1965. Cover, biomass and root/shoot habit of *Larrea divaricata* on a selected site in southern New Mexico. Thesis, New Mexico State University, Las Cruces.

Solbrig, O. T. 1977. The adaptive strategies of *Larrea*, pp. 1–9. *In:* T. J. Mabry, J. H. Hunziker, D. R. Difeo (eds.). Creosote bush. Biology and chemistry of *Larrea* in new world deserts. Dowden, Hutchinson, and Ross; Stroudsburg, Pennsylvania.

Sternberg, L. 1976. Growth forms of *Larrea tridentata*. Madrono 23:408–417.

Stearns, S. C. 1976. Life-history tactics: A review of the ideas. The Quarterly Review of Biology 51:3–47.

Strain, B. R., and V. C. Chase. 1966. Effect of past and prevailing temperatures on the carbon dioxide exchange capacities of some woody desert perennials. Ecology 47:1043–1045.

Strain, B. R. 1969. Seasonal adaptation in photosynthesis and respiration in four desert shrubs growing in situ. Ecology 50:511–513.

Stribley, D. P., D. J. Read, and R. Hunt. 1975. The biology of mycorrhiiza in the Ericacean. V. The effects of myocrrhizal infection, soil type and partial soil-sterilization on the growth of cranberry (Vaccinium macrocarpon Ait.). New Phytologist 75:119–130.

Taylor, S. E. 1975. Optimal leaf form, pp. 73–86. In: D. M. Gates and R. B. Schmerl (eds.). Perspectives of biophysical ecology, Springer-Verlag, New York.

Thomas, J. E., C. D. Raper, and W. W. Weeks. 1981. Day and night temperature effects on N and soluble carbohydrate allocation during early reproductive growth in soybeans. Agronomy Journal 73:577–582.

Thompson, A. C., H. C. Lane, J. W. Jones, and J. D. Hesketh. 1976. N concentrations of cotton leaves, buds, and bolls in relation to age and N fertilization. Agronomy Journal 68:617–621.

Thornley, J. H. M. 1972a. A model to describe the partitioning of photosynthate during vegetative plant growth. Annals of Botany 36:419–430.

Thornley, J. H. M. 1972b. A balanced quantitative model for root:shoot ratios in vegetative plants. Annals of Botany 36:431–441.

Thornley, J. H. M. 1976. Mathematical models in plant physiology. Academic Press, London.

Thornley, J. H. M. 1977. Root:shoot interactions. Symposium of the Society of Experimental Biology 31:367–389.

Troughton, A. 1977. The rate of growth and partitioning of assimilates in young grass plants: a mathematical model. Annals of Botany 41:533–565.

Trumble, H. C., and K. Woodroffe. 1954. The influence of climatic factors on the reaction of desert shrubs to grazing by sheep. In: J. L. Cloudsley-Thompson (ed.). Biology of deserts, Institute of Biology, London.

Vanderlip, R. L., and G. J. Arkin. 1977. Simulating accumulation and distribution of dry matter in grain sorghum. Agronomy Journal 69:917–923.

van Keulen, H. 1981. Modelling the interaction of water and nitrogen. Plant and Soil 58:205–229.

Vasek, F. C. 1980. Creosote bush: Long-lived clones in the Mojave desert. American Journal of Botany 76:246–255.

Wallace, A., E. M. Romney, and R. T. Aschcroft. 1970. Soil temperature effects on growth of seedlings of some shrub species which grow in the transitional area between the Mojave and Great Basin deserts. BioScience 20:1158–1159.

Wallace, A., and E. M. Romney. 1972. Radioecology and ecophysiology of desert plants at the Nevada test site. USAEC Report TID-25954.

Wallace, A., E. M. Romney, and J. W. Cha. 1980a. Persistence of ^{14}C labeled carbon in Larrea tridentata up to 40 months after photosynthetic fixation in the northern Mojave Desert. Great Basin Naturalist Memoirs 4:177–199.

Wallace, A., R. T. Mueller, J. W. Cha, and E. M. Romney. 1980b. ^{14}C distribution in roots following photosynthesis of the label in perennial plants in the northern Mojave Desert. Great Basin Naturalist Memoirs 4:192–200.

Wallace, A., J. W. Cha, and E. M. Romney. 1980c. Distribution of photosynthetically fixed ^{14}C in perennial plant species of the northern Mojave Desert. Great Basin Naturalist Memoirs 4:192–200.

Wann, M., and C. D. Raper. 1979. A dynamic model for plant growth: adaptation for vegetative growth of soybeans. Crop Science 19:461–467.

Wareing, P. F., and J. Patrick. 1975. Source-sink relations and the partition of assimilates in the plant, pp. 481–499. *In:* J. P. Cooper (ed.). Photosynthesis and productivity in different environments, Cambridge University Press, London.

West, N. E. 1981. Nutrient cycling in desert ecosystems, pp. 301–324. *In:* D. W. Goodall, and R. A. Perry (eds.). Arid land ecosystems: Structure, functioning and management, Vol. 2, Cambridge University Press, London.

Whittaker, R. H. 1970. Communities and ecosystems. MacMillan Press, New York.

Whittaker, R. H., and W. A. Niering. 1975. Vegetation of the Santa Catalina Mountains, Arizona. V. Biomass, production, and diversity along the elevation gradient. Ecology 56:771–790.

Wilkerson, G. G., J. W. Jones, K. T. Ingram, and J. W. Mishoe. 1981. Modeling soybean growth for crop management. Proceedings of the American Society of Agricultural Engineers, Paper No. 81-4014.

Williams, L. E., T. M. DeJong, and D. A. Phillips. 1981. Carbon and nitrogen limitation on soybean seedling development. Plant Physiology 68:1208–1209.

Williams, R. B., and K. L. Bell. 1981. Nitrogen allocation in Mojave Desert annuals. Oecologia 48:145–150.

Williams, W. E. 1983. Optimal water-use efficiency in a California shrub. Plant, Cell and Environment 6:145–151.

Wilson, B. F. 1975. Distribution of secondary thickening in tree root systems, pp. 197–219. *In:* J. G. Torrey, and D. T. Clarkson (eds.). The development and function of roots, Academic Press, London.

3

THE ROLES OF VERTEBRATES IN DESERT ECOSYSTEMS

James H. Brown

University of Arizona
Tucson, Arizona

INTRODUCTION

Probably because among all the organisms with which we share this planet we ourselves are vertebrates, we seem especially interested in the biology of vertebrate animals and exceptionally concerned about the continued survival of their populations. Perhaps, in part, to justify our preoccupation with these animals and the feelings of kinship and beauty which they elicit, we would like to think that vertebrates play important roles in the greater scheme of things. We would like to identify and understand these ecological roles.

Deserts are a good place to begin. Compared to other ecosystems, deserts are relatively simple and easy to study. Relative to other kinds of organisms, vertebrates are probably as diverse, abundant, and conspicuous in deserts as they are in most other ecosystems. Productivity of desert habitats is not only low, but it also occurs in infrequent, unpredictable pulses that are caused by variation in the availability of limited water (see, for example, Noy-Meir 1973, 1974). Consequently, the supply of food for vertebrates is scanty and irregular. Largely for these reasons, deserts and their vertebrate biotas have been the subject of much study. We have learned a good deal about the structure and dynamics of desert ecosystems and about the organismic and population biology of desert vertebrates. Unfortunately, we still know very little about the roles of different kinds of desert vertebrates, and by definition each species occupies its own unique ecological niche.

In the chapter, rather than attempting to provide definitive answers, I hope to focus on the kinds of questions and approaches that might prove useful in increasing our understanding of the roles of vertebrates in desert ecosystems. The desert vertebrates can be divided into functional ecological groups based largely on shared traits at the organismic level. These combinations of morphological, physiological, and behavioral characteristics are intimately related to the kind of ecological niche each species occupies. Thus, it should be possible to predict the ecological roles of different groups from their organismic level traits, to frame these predictions as testable hypotheses, and to test these hypotheses with appropriate observations and experiments. I shall illustrate this approach by describing some of the effects of seed-eating mammals and birds on desert ecosystems that have been demonstrated by our recent experimental work. I shall conclude that vertebrates probably have major regulatory effects on the structure and function of desert ecosystems, but only a few of these roles have yet been documented rigorously.

Throughout the chapter I shall confine my attention to those vertebrates which occur in arid terrestrial habitats in the deserts of southwestern North America. Most extensive desert regions contain patches of agricultural, riparian, and aquatic habitats, and these support distinctive vertebrate biotas; however, I do not regard these habitats as desert and I shall not consider their inhabitants further. Most of the major taxonomic and functional groups of vertebrates found in North American deserts also occur in other major desert regions of the world where they probably occupy similar ecological niches. But this is a gross generalization to which there are many exceptions. In certain deserts some groups of vertebrates play conspicuously different ecological roles, whereas other groups are greatly reduced or absent and their niches either go unfilled or are filled by other kinds of organisms. Unfortunately, we know far less about these other deserts and their vertebrate faunas than we do about their North American counterparts.

A DESERT BESTIARY

This section identifies the important kinds of desert vertebrates and classifies them in functional ecological groups. To the extent that this classification recognizes the four classes of terrestrial vertebrates (amphibians, reptiles, birds, and mammals) as separate categories, it is also taxonomic. This simply emphasizes that members of each class share morphological, physiological, and behavioral traits that have important ecological consequences.

Amphibians.   A few kinds of amphibians, especially representatives of the anuran genera *Scaphiopus* and *Bufo*, spend most of their adult lives in truly arid habitats, although they require at least temporary water for breeding and larval development. Very little is known about the terrestrial ecology of these amphibians. They are neither abundant nor conspicuous in most desert habitats, and their activity is strictly confined to infrequent wet periods. For these reasons, I suspect that the roles of these amphibians in desert systems are inconsequential or modest, especially when compared to the roles of the other groups considered below. Obviously, this is only the first of many topics that requires further investigation.

Reptiles. Reptiles, especially lizards and snakes, are diverse and abundant in deserts. Much of their success can be attributed to a suite of traits that enable them to play ecological roles very different from those of birds and mammals. Unlike endotherms, which use internal heat production to maintain high, relatively constant body temperatures, reptiles are ectothermic; their body temperature varies with the thermal characteristics of their environment. Most desert reptiles require a narrow range of relatively high (>30°C) body temperatures for normal activity, and they employ behavioral mechanisms, such as basking, to attain these activity temperatures. This means, however, that their activity is restricted to those times of day and seasons of the year when environmental temperature regimes permit such behavioral thermoregulation. Associated with these differences in thermoregulatory and activity patterns, reptiles have much lower energy requirements than those of birds and mammals. Even at comparable body temperatures (30–40°C) standard resting metabolic rates of ectothermic reptiles and amphibians are only 10 to 20% those of endothermic vertebrates of comparable size (Bennett and Dawson 1976, Feder 1976). Since desert reptiles spend substantial parts of their daily and annual cycles inactive and at much lower body temperatures, their long-term rates of energy intake are even lower, perhaps only 1 to 5% those of birds and mammals of comparable size (Bennett and Nagy 1977, Pough 1980).

These physiological and behavioral traits of individual reptiles have profound ecological consequences. A habitat or food resource that could sustain only a small population of birds or mammals can support a much larger population of lizards, snakes, or tortoises. Thus, reptiles are ecologically more efficient than endotherms in the sense that a much larger proportion of the food they consume is incorporated into biomass and made available to their predators at higher trophic levels. Available data suggest that ectotherms are at least an order of magnitude more efficient as producers of biomass than are birds and mammals of comparable size (McNeill and Lawton 1970, Turner 1970, Humphreys 1979). Furthermore, the reptiles can go dormant and survive for many months without eating food. As long as the periods of availability of food resources correspond with temperature regimes that are suitable for activity, reptiles can be successful in desert ecosystems. Their diversity and abundance can be attributed, in large part, to low productivity that favors organisms with low food requirements and to the widely fluctuating climatic conditions that enable ectotherms to seek out low temperatures, remain inactive, and conserve energy, and to emerge and be active only when environmental temperatures and food supplies are favorable.

The traits indicated above are generally characteristic of all desert reptiles. Additional attributes can be used to divide them into three functional ecological groups.

1. Small insectivores. Most of the species and individuals of desert reptiles are small lizards and snakes that feed primarily on invertebrates. This group includes the smallest of the desert vertebrates; most adult individuals weigh from 1 to 50 g. The most abundant and conspicuous of these reptiles are the diurnal iguanid and teiid lizards. Most of the former (for example, *Sceloporus*, *Uta*, and *Phrynosoma*) are intermittently active, sit-and-wait predators, whereas the latter (for example, *Cnemidophorus*) are more continuously moving, searching hunters. In addition to these, however, there is a substantial but poorly studied fauna of nocturnal lizards (for example, *Coleonyx* and *Xantusia*) and small, usually nocturnal snakes (for example, *Leptotyphlops*, *Phyllorhynchus*, *Rhinocheilus*, *Sonora*, *Chionactis*, *Chilomeniscus*, *Ficimia*, and *Tantilla*).

2. Large carnivores. This group includes the larger snakes (for example, *Masticophis*, *Pituophis*, *Lampropeltis*, *Salvadora*, *Arizona*, *Trimorphodon*, *Hypsiglena*, *Crotalus*) and a few large lizards (for example, *Heloderma* and *Crotaphytus*). These mostly weigh from 50 g to 2 kg and feed on other vertebrates. Some of the snakes and the large lizards are diurnal and feed primarily on lizards (*Heloderma* eats birds' eggs), whereas other snakes are nocturnal and many of them prey mostly on small mammals.

3. Large folivores. This final group includes the few desert reptiles that feed primarily on plant material. It contains a few large lizards (for example, *Dipsosaurus* and *Sauromalus*) and the desert tortoises (*Gopherus*). These reptiles weigh approximately 50 g to 2 kg; they are all diurnal, and they feed mostly on leaves but also on flowers and fruits when they are available.

Birds. Unlike the other groups of desert vertebrates, relatively few kinds of birds are restricted to desert habitats. On the other hand, many species, representing several families and orders, occur in deserts as either permanent residents or migrants. As a group, birds share several attributes that greatly influence their ecological roles.

First, they are endothermic. They maintain high, relatively constant body temperatures. This is associated with high rates of metabolism, and with high levels of foraging and activity. A very few desert birds, including hummingbirds and swifts, can reduce energy expenditure during periods of low food supply by allowing their body temperatures to drop to near ambient levels at night when they are inactive. Another species, the poorwill (*Phalaenoptilus nuttallii*), is known to hibernate with a low body temperature and without feeding for several winter months. But these are exceptions. The vast majority of desert birds must have high, relatively constant rates of food intake throughout the year.

A second general attribute of birds is their ability to fly. The mobility conferred by flight enables birds to avoid many of the problems of continually meeting high energy requirements in an environment of low and fluctuating food resources. The temporal and spatial scale of movement varies among species, but almost all desert birds use their mobility to track food supplies. Many species are migratory; they are not permanent residents of arid habitats, but move into them only during seasons when sufficient food resources are available. These and other species also travel considerable distances within deserts to locate and exploit locally abundant foods (see, for example, Raitt and Pimm 1976, Pulliam and Parker 1979, Dunning and Brown 1982). Even on a daily basis, many birds commute regularly between desert and adjacent agricultural, riparian, or other kinds of habitats to meet requirements not only for food, but also for water and breeding and roosting sites.

Another trait characteristic of desert birds is great variability and flexibility in diet and foraging behavior. Switching facultatively to utilize alternative food sources as they become available appears to characterize most species, but it is particularly important in enabling some of the permanent resident species to persist in an environment that is highly seasonal as well as unproductive. This switching tends to blur the distinctions between some of the dietary categories below. Many of the species which are generally regarded as insectivorous feed heavily on seeds during winter months when invertebrates are inactive, and conversely, otherwise granivorous and frugivorous species take many insects during warm periods when such foods are available.

Despite this flexibility, it is possible to divide the desert birds into three functional groups, as follows.

1. Small insectivores. This taxonomically diverse assemblage contains many species with body weights in the range of 4 to 80 g. It includes the diurnal woodpeckers, flycatchers, wrens, phainopeplas, verdins, and

shrikes; the crepuscular goatsuckers; and the small nocturnal owls. Although all of these feed primarily on insects, they exhibit a wide variety of foraging behaviors, including aerial hawking, sallying, foliage gleaning, and ground and trunk foraging. Rather than executing a special category for the few species of nectar-feeding hummingbirds, they are included here because they also feed, to a large extent, on insects.

2. Small granivores. Those birds which feed primarily on seeds are diurnal, weigh from 10 to 200 g, and belong to three groups: the finches, doves, and quail. The finches take seeds primarily in the winter, when migrant sparrows join the resident sparrows, house finches, and towhees. The sparrows often form mixed-species flocks and forage over large areas. Doves and quail tend to be present throughout the year, although they may move around within the deserts.

3. Large carnivores. This group contains the large nocturnal owls and the diurnal hawks, eagles, ravens, and roadrunners. These are relatively large birds, weighing from 100 g to 5 kg. They take a variety of prey, including lizards, snakes, other birds, and small mammals.

Mammals.   Many diverse kinds of mammals are remarkably abundant in deserts, even though they lack both the energy efficient ectothermy of reptiles and the tremendous mobility of birds (except for bats, of course). All mammals are basically endothermic, and most species, like birds, require sustained high levels of food intake to support their high metabolic rates. There are some important exceptions. Many species of rodents or bats either hibernate or estivate. During seasons when food is unavailable they become inactive, allow their body temperatures to drop to near ambient levels, and drastically reduce their energy requirements.

Perhaps the single trait which contributes most importantly to the success of mammals, as a group, in desert habitats is the amazing sophistication of their foraging behavior. This can take many forms. The small omnivores and large carnivores exhibit highly flexible diets and associated foraging strategies. Like many birds, they readily switch among alternative food types, depending on their availability. Other species, such as the small seed-eating rodents and larger foliage-eating rodents and lagomorphs have highly restricted diets and specialized foraging behaviors. Although the populations of these dietary specialists fluctuate to some extent with variation in their food supply (see, for example, French et al. 1974, Whitford 1976), individuals manage to find sufficient food to survive even the toughest times. Some species, especially the granivores, store large quantities of food. By harvesting food when it is abundant and hoarding it for use when it is scarce, they avoid much of the potentially adverse effect of depending on a widely and unpredictably fluctuating food supply.

In many ecologically relevant traits, such as body size, diet, and mode of locomotion, mammals are much more diverse than any other class of desert vertebrates. This is reflected in the designation of six functional groups of desert mammals, twice as many categories as were erected for either reptiles or birds.

1. Small granivores. This group is perhaps the richest in species but the most homogeneous in their attributes. It is composed exclusively of small (7–120 g), nocturnal rodents of the families Heteromyidae (*Dipodomys, Microdipodops*, and *Perognathus*) and Cricetidae (*Reithrodontomys* and *Peromyscus*). These burrowing rodents exist largely or exclusively on the seeds of desert plants. The heteromyid species are particularly avid hoarders. Functional diversity within this group includes variation in mode of locomotion (*Dipodomys* and *Microdipodops* are bipedal and saltatorial, whereas the others are quadrupedal and scansorial), in seasonal activity (*Microdipodops* and *Perognathus* hibernate and the others remain active throughout the year, although a few species may enter torpor occasionally), and in their capacity to subsist on a diet consisting exclusively of dry seeds (most of the heteromyids can, whereas the cricetids probably require some additional free water, which they obtain from eating some insects or green vegetation).

2. Small to medium-sized folivores. This group includes several kinds of rodents (*Spermophilus, Neotoma, Thomomys*) and lagamorphs (*Sylvilagus* and *Lepus*). These grazers and browsers span a fairly wide range of body sizes (100 g to 1 kg), are both diurnal and nocturnal, and include hibernators (*Spermophilus*) and fossorial species (*Thomomys*).

3. Small to medium-sized omnivores. Most representatives of this group are small (15–100 g) rodents of the genera *Peromyscus, Onychomys*, and *Ammospermophilus*. Most of these are primarily insectivorous, but they take large numbers of seeds and fruits, especially in cold seasons when invertebrates are inactive. The much larger (200 g–5 kg), primarily insectivorous skunks (*Mephitis, Conepeatus*, and *Spilogale*) and the tiny (3.5 g), almost exclusively insectivorous desert shrew (*Notiosorex*) should probably be included with this group.

4. Large carnivores. Aside from the skunks, most desert representatives of the order Carnivora (for example, *Bassariscus, Urocyon, Vulpes, Canis, Taxidea*, and *Lynx*) prey extensively on small mammals. Members of this group are primarily nocturnal. They range in body weight from 1 to 5 kg. Although I classify these mammals as carnivores, many of them, especially the foxes and coyotes, feed heavily on fruits and invertebrates when these items are abundant or when vertebrate prey are in short supply.

5. Large folivores. This group includes the native grazers and browsers in the order Artiodactyla (for example, peccary, mule deer, bighorn sheep,

and pronghorn antelope). These animals weigh from 10 to 100 kg, are active both day and night, and are sufficiently mobile to migrate substantial distances on a seasonal basis. To these must be added domestic sheep, goats, cattle, burros, and horses. Most North American desert habitats have been grazed by substantial populations of either tended or feral livestock, and the impact of these animals on the ecosystem as a whole has probably been at least as large as that of any other group of vertebrates. One can only speculate about the equally great influence potentially of the Pleistocene megafauna (including ground sloths, camels, and horses) which grazed these same deserts until they became extinct only a few thousand years ago (see, for example, Martin and Wright 1967).

6. Bats. In addition to being members of the single order, Chiroptera, desert bats form a functionally homogeneous group. They are all small (3–20 g), nocturnal, and highly mobile. Most of the bats (for example, *Pipistrellus*, *Antrozous*, and *Tadarida*) are exclusively insectivorous, although nectar- and pollen-eating forms (*Choeronycteris* and *Leptonycteris*) occur in some habitats. Like birds, bats are highly mobile, and they occur in most desert habitats only during seasons when insects and flowers are abundant.

ECOLOGICAL ROLES

Several investigators have observed that all of the vertebrates together account for only a tiny proportion (usually on the order of 1% or less) of the number of individuals, biomass, and flows of energy and matter in natural ecosystems (see, for example, Golley 1973, Chew 1974; Petrusewicz et al. 1974). Deserts appear to be no exception (Chew and Chew 1970, Noy-Meir 1974). Thus, these authors and others have concluded that if vertebrates influence importantly the structure and function of ecosystems they must have what have come to be called regulatory effects. Rather than contributing importantly directly to the processes of energy flow and nutrient cycling, vertebrates could have major impact on critical ecosystem components and processes. By differentially affecting certain other species or features of the nonliving environment, which, in turn, influence still other components, vertebrates could have direct qualitative effects that become quantitatively important as they are amplified through the system by further interactions.

Vertebrates have three distinct kinds of direct effects on ecosystems: as predators, they consume other organisms; as prey, they produce food for their own predators, parasites, and decomposers; and as mechanical processors, they move objects around and change their physical form. If any of these activities are highly selective and directed at key ecosystems components that themselves have important quantitative or qualitative effects, vertebrates probably have much more influence on the structure and function of ecosystems than is suggested by their relatively inconsequential numbers, biomass, and energy flow.

Consumption. As suggested by the brief characterizations of diets in the previous section, almost all organic materials except wood, detritus, and microorganisms are consumed by desert vertebrates. Most kinds of foods are eaten by more than one functional group: green vegetation by large reptiles, small mammals, and large mammals; seeds by small birds and small mammals; insects by small reptiles, small birds, small terrestrial mammals, and bats; vertebrates by large reptiles, large birds, and large mammals; and nectar by small birds and bats. This apparent overlap in diet means that different taxonomic and functional groups of vertebrates compete potentially for limited food resources in unproductive desert environments. (The vertebrates also compete potentially with invertebrates that consume these same resources.)

On the other hand, the different functional groups and different species within the same functional group use similar food resources in different ways. Many of these differences are obvious, or at least they could be predicted from the organic level traits of the members of the various functional groups. Foraging strategies must be adequate to meet the energy requirements for survival and reproduction. The food requirements depend most importantly on the body size of the individuals and whether they are ectothermic reptiles or endothermic birds and mammals. Patterns of daily and seasonal activity determine temporal patterns of resource utilization, whereas mobility and foraging behavior influence the spatial patterns of food harvesting. The constraints of different nutritive requirements, searching, and handling cause each species to forage selectively for different kinds of food items. Taken together, these differences among species and functional groups presumably enable each species to sustain its population and to coexist with other members of the community despite some competition with certain other species for shared food resources.

Another consequence of the variation in foraging strategies among species and functional groups is the selective impact of different kinds of vertebrates on particular prey species. In order to meet their high energy requirements for survival and reproduction and to compete successfully for shared food resources with invertebrates and other kinds of vertebrates, all members of all functional groups must be efficient, highly selective foragers. Much of the behavior of vertebrates, especially of endothermic birds and mammals, represents adaptations for economically harvesting energy resources that are dispersed in time, in space, and among prey species that vary in suitability and availability. The recent development of optimal foraging theory and its success in accounting for the many aspects of vertebrate searching and feeding behavior (see Pyke et al. 1977) reflect the realization that animals have been strongly selected to increase the effectiveness of their foraging by hunting in certain places and by selectively searching for and pursuing not only certain prey species but often even particular life history stages of those species. Such selective predation must affect prey species differentially, changing their abundances and distributions, and altering the outcome of their interactions with still other species.

Production.   Vertebrates not only consume many kinds of organisms; they, in turn, are preyed upon by a variety of carnivores and parasites, and their remains provide sustenance for scavengers, detritivores, and decomposers. Many of the species which consume vertebrates are specialists that are dependent on vertebrate prey for their own survival. These consumers, however, must be even less important than the vertebrate producers in the quantitative flow of energy and materials through the ecosystem. From the comments made earlier, it is apparent that ectothermic reptiles are much more efficient producers than endothermic birds and mammals. That is, reptiles incorporate a much greater proportion (by a factor of at least 10) of their own food into biomass that is then available to predators. On the other hand, the populations of predators that actually are supported will depend on the abundances and availabilities of prey. In many desert habitats birds and mammals may support as many or more consumers than reptiles, simply because they are at least as abundant and they are available throughout the year. Clearly, many of the higher links in desert food webs are partially or totally dependent on vertebrate food resources, but in order to evaluate the roles of vertebrates as producers in desert ecosystems much more information on these relationships must be obtained.

Mechanical processing.   Vertebrates are among the largest and most active of desert organisms. They can play potentially important roles by transporting objects and by changing the physical nature of materials. Although the magnitude of these activities may not compare with abiotic physical events (such as air and water movement and tectonic events) because of the precision and predictability of their behavior, the mechanical effects of vertebrates may be no less important. Perhaps this is most clearly evidenced by pollinators. Certain birds and bats are the primary, often obligate pollinators of many desert plants, including some of the dominant shrubs and succulents. Clearly, the transport of plant gametes plays a significant role in maintaining the present organization of ecosystems. Other vertebrates, especially the highly mobile birds and large mammals, are important dispersers of seeds.

During the processing of food, all vertebrates transform and transport materials. When they deposit feces and urine, they leave physically altered organic and inorganic substances in new locations, sometimes far from where they were produced and ingested. Other species do not even ingest much of the organic material that they harvest while foraging. For example, jackrabbits (*Lepus*) cut tremendous quantities of living twigs from certain species of shrubs (for example, *Larrea* and *Gutierrezia*) and then consume only tiny amounts of selected leaves or bark (see Steinberger and Whitford, 1983). Similarly, many desert rodents undoubtedly collect and store far more seeds than they subsequently eat. These vertebrates must have much greater impact as predators on living plants than would ever be estimated from their energy budgets.

Vertebrates also process and modify soil. Many of the small mammals are burrowers, and their extensive digging activities mix the soil and alter its physical properties. Pocket gophers (*Thomomys*), which have been shown to have important impacts on other ecosystems by their tunneling (Grinnell 1923, Mielke, 1977, Grant et al. 1980), are present and may play similar roles in most desert habitats with friable soils. Other rodents (for example, *Neotoma* and some *Dipodomys*) construct elaborate nests or burrows that serve as important breeding sites or refuges for other animal species. These rodents also transport large quantities of organic material to their dens, which then become highly concentrated sources of decomposing detritus (Steinberger and Whitford, 1983).

VERTEBRATES AS REGULATORS

If vertebrates are quantitatively insignificant in the numbers of individuals, biomass, and flows of energy and materials through ecosystems, they can still have major effects if they have a highly selective impact on key elements and processes, especially if these, in turn, have similar kinds of effects on still other components. Certainly, the organismic level traits of vertebrates suggest that they might play such roles. The ecological consequences of these traits can be examined to formulate hypotheses about the potential effects of different functional groups of vertebrates in desert ecosystems.

Predictions. Because of their high energy requirements and highly selective foraging behaviors, vertebrates are particularly likely to influence the organization of ecosystems through their activities as consumers. Although roles of vertebrates as producers and physical processors warrant further study, they will not be developed further in the present paper except to note that most of the physical processing activities are closely associated with feeding.

It is possible to imagine two major consequences of selective foraging on the functional organization of ecosystems. On the one hand, selective consumers have differential impacts on other populations, both on producers that can serve as alternative prey and on other consumers with overlapping food requirements that are competitors. Since the affected species probably interact with still other species, the influence of a single species or functional group can potentially spread and be amplified through the ecosystem by means of such indirect interactions. If these kinds of regulatory effects are important, we can expect major differences in the internal organization of ecosystems, depending on what kinds of vertebrate consumers are present. If important species or functional groups are removed experimentally, we predict substantial changes in patterns of dominance and species composition. On the other hand, selective consumers have compensating responses that tend to maintain a homeostasis of structure and function of the entire ecosystem in the face of internal or external perturbations. Interspecific competition is one such compensatory process. If two species have overlapping requirements for limiting resources, then if one population declines and consumes less, the other increases and consumes more. This tends to maintain the availability of resources and the flows of energy and matter at relatively constant levels when both species are present, because each can compensate for perturbations in the abundance and consumption rate of the other. Similarly, a weblike trophic structure, in which most predators have several alternative prey species, encourages selectively switching consumption that tends to check differential increases in particular producer populations and to maintain a homeostasis of prey species composition and of rates of energy and matter transfer. Thus, vertebrates can regulate ecosystems in two ways: they can influence the species composition by selectively regulating the exchange of energy and materials among species, and they can do this in such a way as to maintain homeostasis of the ecosystem as a whole.

In general, I would expect all species and functional groups of vertebrates to have both kinds of regulatory effects, although the exact nature and magnitude of their impacts should vary. Vertebrate consumers probably influence species composition both by competing with other consumers and by regulating populations of their prey. Because of wide overlaps in diet, there is probably substantial interspecific competition among species within functional groups, between different functional groups, and between vertebrates and other organisms. The organization of these communities of consumers with overlapping food requirements should depend importantly on what kinds of vertebrate competitors are present. Experimental removal of particular species or functional groups should change the availability of resources to the remaining species, benefit some of them differentially, and cause changes in their relative abundances which will probably lead to secondary effects on other species with which these species interact.

As selective predators, vertebrates regulate the abundance and distribution of at least some prey species. The suitability of alternative prey varies, with the result that selective consumers differentially limit the density and spatial distribution of preferred prey species. The regulatory effects of such selective predation interact with competition among prey species and with predation by other kinds of predators (including invertebrates) on the same prey to influence the relative abundance and distribution of producer species.

Some of the possible kinds of effects can be illustrated by a specific example. Vertebrate grazers and browsers should be highly selective croppers. Not all plants are equally palatable and nutritious. Folivores can reduce the time that they are exposed to their own predators and increase the rate of acquisition of the energy and materials necessary for their survival and reproduction by feeding on a selected subset of available plant species (and also probably by feeding in certain habitats and microhabitats and perhaps by selecting only particular parts of individual plants). This selective foraging limits the growth and reproduction of preferred species. It also makes limited resources (such as water, nutrients, and light) available to the other plant species that are not eaten because they possess chemical or physical defenses that make them unpalatable or phenologies that make them unavailable. Since these antipredator strategies presumably involve costs of predator avoidance, those plants which possess them should be more inferior competitors than the preferred food species in the absence of vertebrate herbivores. This leads to a clearly testable prediction: if vertebrate grazers and browsers are removed experimentally, their preferred food plants should increase in relative dominance in the plant community.

The compensatory effects of vertebrate consumers potentially have homeostatic influences. Natural history observations indicate much overlap in the diets of different species and even different functional groups. Many groups also exhibit extremely flexible diets, readily shifting not only among alternative prey species of the same general type but even switching between very different kinds of food (such as invertebrates and seeds) depending on availability. These are the kinds of traits required for vertebrates to play a significant role in regulating ecosystem processes such as energy flow at relatively constant levels: constant at least relative to the drastically fluctuating productivity caused by the infrequent and unpredictable availability of limited water. Thus, we can predict that if we perturb an ecosystem by artificially increasing the availability of some food resource or decreasing the population of some kind of consumer, then some kinds of vertebrates will compensate by increasing their consumption and preventing the accumulation of unused resources. Of course, ability to compensate in this way will be limited by constraints on such traits as mode of locomotion and the behavioral capacity to harvest and physiological capacity to obtain sustenance from different kinds of food items. Maximal compensation may occur only in evolutionary time when organisms are able to adapt to different patterns of resource availability. An apparent example of such evolutionary compensation is the different, sometimes convergent ecological roles played by representatives of the three classes of vertebrates in the major deserts of the world. For example, there are major differences in biomass, population density, and species diversity of functional groups of reptiles, birds, and mammals between North American and Australian deserts (Pianka 1973, Morton 1979, Brown et al. 1979).

Although all selective consumers should have these same general kinds of regulatory effects, the exact nature and magnitude of the impact will vary among species and functional groups. In general, birds and mammals, foraging to meet their higher individual food requirements, should have greater regulatory effects than reptiles that consume the same kinds of food resources. This is complicated, however, by the fact that different groups forage on different spatial and temporal scales. Because vertebrates as a group are highly mobile and can concentrate their foraging on locally available prey, their general effect should be to reduce spatial variability in preferred food resources. With their great mobility, birds should be especially effective on large spatial scales, whereas mammals, with their great food-finding ability, should have similar impacts within local habitats. Although vertebrate foraging tends to reduce spatial variability, it probably increases temporal variation in the availability of preferred food resources. Production in deserts occurs in infrequent, unpredictable pulses that are determined by the availability of limited water for plant growth. By harvesting food efficiently soon after it is produced, vertebrates must contribute importantly to the rapid depletion of resources and the feast-and-famine pattern of food availability.

Using the organismic level attributes of the different functional groups, it is possible to make predictions about their roles as consumers. The most mobile vertebrates—birds, bats, and large terrestrial mammals—are "cream skimmers." They rely on their mobility to search over large areas and to locate and exploit large patches of relatively abundant food produced in response to recent precipitation. On the other hand, reptiles and small terrestrial mammals must remain within local areas and tolerate the drastic fluctuations in food resources. Reptiles would seem to be in an especially advantageous position. Most of them, as well as some hibernating and estivating mammals, are active only at certain seasons when food tends to be available. Furthermore, even when they are maximally active, reptiles require much less food than endotherms of comparable size. Therefore, reptiles can be substantially less efficient foragers and still obtain sufficient food to coexist with competing birds and mammals. Small mammals must use different strategies to obtain food and compete successfully with birds and reptiles. Folivores use resources eaten not at all by birds and by only a very few kinds of reptiles. Granivores store seeds when they are available and use them when food is scarce. Omnivores, which would seem to have the greatest problem, have such flexible diets and good food-finding ability that they manage to find enough to eat even in the toughest times. In addition, the functional groups differ importantly in life history traits, which cause their populations to respond differently to fluctuations in food supply.

Testing hypotheses.   Although potential effects of vertebrate consumers can be predicted from considerations of foraging behavior, diet, energy requirements, mobility, and other organismic traits, the actual impact of different species and functional groups on other elements of the ecosystem can best be assessed by manipulative experiments. This is particularly true of indirect effects; those caused by vertebrates affecting some ecosystem components directly and these, in turn, influencing other elements.

Perhaps the most informative experiments, at least initially, will also be the most obvious ones: those in which a single species or entire functional group is removed and the structure and function of the manipulated ecosystem is compared with an unmanipulated control. Such experiments are admittedly crude. They are analogous in many ways to ablation experiments in physiology: To determine the function of an endocrine gland or a part of the central nervous system, the organ in question is removed surgically and the responses of treated individuals are compared with sham-operated controls. These kinds of experiments continue to play central roles in the development of endocrinology and neurophysiology, although they have serious limitations. In both physiology and ecosystem ecology, removal experiments are useful for detecting the general effects of particular elements on the structure and function of complex systems, but they are of limited value in understanding normal steady-state function of the components, especially their interactions with other regulatory elements. Our present knowledge of the roles of vertebrates in ecosystems is rudimentary. As we begin to appreciate the nature and magnitude of the effects of removing particular kinds of vertebrates, we will be in a better position to design more sophisticated experiments to further elucidate their functional roles.

One of the great advantages of desert ecosystems for such experimentation is the relative ease with which they can be manipulated in controlled and informative ways. A potential problem with all artificial manipulation is the creation of experimental artifacts, the unanticipated side effects of human intervention that can lead to erroneous interpretations. This is a major problem for ecologists because the biocides, trapping programs, and exclosures that are required to maintain the exclusion of particular kinds of organisms may have great, unanticipated effects on other components of the ecosystem. The simple physical structure and limited species diversity of desert ecosystems make it possible to remove selected species and entire functional groups with almost surgical precision. Because there are relatively few other organisms, the extent to which these might be affected by experimental artifacts is limited, and additional controls can be designed to ensure against such side effects.

An example: experiments with granivores. Recent experiments with desert seed-eaters by my collaborators and myself not only illustrate the kinds of regulatory effects different functional groups can have; they also demonstrate the power of simple removal experiments to give interesting insights into these roles.

Our first set of experiments were begun in 1973 and largely discontinued in 1977, when a new, more elaborate series was initiated. Some results, especially those of the earlier experiments, have already been published; but much of the work is still in progress, analyses are incomplete, and many of the results described below must be regarded as preliminary. Our manipulations involve removing some or all species of granivorous rodents and ants and adding supplemental seed to large plots of Sonoran and Chihuahuan Desert. We have monitored effects of these treatments and appropriate controls on rodents, ants, birds, and annual plants. In the present summary, I shall concentrate on the vertebrates: on the effects of removing rodents, and on the responses of rodents and birds to the experimental manipulations.

There is abundant evidence that seeds are a limiting resource for granivores, and that competition for food plays an important role in the functional organization of the granivore community. Removal of rodents resulted in substantial increases in the number of colonies of granivorous ants; reciprocal removal of ants resulted in less pronounced increases in the density of seed-eating rodents (Brown and Davidson 1977, Brown et al. 1979, Bryant et al. 1976). Small seed-eating rodents (four species) increased at least 300% in density in response to the exclusion of three species of larger rodents (Munger and Brown 1981). One species of rodent, *Dipodomys spectabilis*, increased dramatically in response to the addition of seeds, but this was accompanied by a decrease in other species, *D. merriami* and *D. ordii*, apparently because of competition (preliminary unpublished results). Birds, especially flocks of finches and doves, foraged more intensely on plots to which supplemental seeds had been added or from which at least some kinds of rodents had been removed than on control plots (preliminary unpublished results). Taken together, these results show that the kinds of seed-eating vertebrates respond differently to experimental manipulations, which affect the availability of seeds, and that they have different effects on other kinds of granivores. In general, vertebrate granivores tend to increase consumption and thus compensate at least partially for increased food availability owing to the removal of other seed predators or the addition of supplementary food.

Seed-eating vertebrates also have major effects as predators on plant populations and communities. Although experiments to examine effects of birds are in progress, most of the available results concern the influence of rodents. When rodents are removed, large-seeded plants increase in density to dominate the annual plant community (Inouye et al. 1980, Inouye 1982). Apparently, when rodents are present, they forage selectively on large seeds, keeping the densities of large-seeded species low. When rodents are removed, large-seeded plants have a competitive advantage over small-seeded species, and they increase to dominate the annual community. This result not only shows that vertebrate seed consumers have important regulatory effects on the producer community; it indicates how such effects can be amplified by secondary interactions, in this case by competition among the producer species.

Inouye (1981) has shown an interesting case in which this kind of amplification is carried one stage further. One of the large-seeded annual plant species that increased dramatically in response to removal of rodents was *Erodium cicutarium*. As density of *E. cicutarium* increased so did the infection rate of a specific fungus, *Synchytrium papillatum*. Thus, rodent removal caused differential increases of certain plant species, one of which differentially affected a specific fungus. The fungus may, in turn, have its own effects. *Synchytrium papillatum* causes high mortality and drastically reduced seed production in *E. cicatarium*, which may lead to yet another series of changes in the plant community and in the specific consumers that utilize the affected and other plant species. In this case the regulatory effects of a functional group of vertebrate consumers has been shown experimentally to reverberate and to be amplified through a desert ecosystem, thereby influencing the structure and function of many aspects of the system.

SUMMARY

An unabashedly speculative evaluation of the ecology of vertebrates leads to the following conclusions about their effects on the structure and function of desert ecosystems.

1. The vertebrates of arid habitats can be divided into several functional groups based on attributes of individual organisms that influence their ecological roles. Among the most important of these traits are mode of temperature regulation (that is, whether ectothermic or endothermic), body size, diet, daily and seasonal activity pattern, and mode of locomotion.

2. Even when all the vertebrates of an ecosystem are considered, their quantitative contribution to the number of individual organisms, biomass, energy flow, and material transfer is very small, usually on the order of 1% of the total for the ecosystem as a whole.

3. Nevertheless, the different kinds of vertebrates affect importantly the structure and function of desert ecosystems because they have highly focused, selected impacts on critical components. These effects can be divided into three functional categories: consumption, production, and mechanical processing. Vertebrates play particularly influential roles as consumers because the different functional groups are highly selective predators on a wide variety of prey species, many of which, in turn, are quantitatively or qualitatively important in the functional organization of desert ecosystem.

4. Vertebrate consumers have two kinds of effects. By feeding selectively on certain prey species, predators alter the abundance, distribution, and species composition of the producers. The influence of such selective predators on the internal organization of ecosystems can be substantial, especially if the affected prey interact importantly, in turn, with still other species. On the other hand, because most vertebrate consumers have highly flexible diets and foraging behaviors, they can compensate for natural perturbations in the availability of food resources and maintain relatively constant flows of energy and materials through the ecosystem as a whole.

5. Although concrete information on the ecosystem-level effects of different functional groups of desert vertebrates is almost nonexistent, ecological roles can be predicted from organismic level traits. In general, endothermic birds and mammals foraging throughout the year to meet higher food requirements should have greater impacts than ectothermic, seasonally active reptiles. Highly mobile birds, bats, and large mammals should reduce spatial variability in prey distribution on a large scale, whereas more sedentary small mammals and reptiles should have similar effects within local patches of habitat. All vertebrates, competing to harvest the most preferred foods when they are available, should contribute to the drastic, unpredictable temporal fluctuations in productivity, biomass, and population density which are ultimately caused by irregular precipitation and are characteristic of all arid regions.

6. Predictions about the roles of vertebrates can best be tested initially by controlled field experiments in which selected species or functional groups are removed from the ecosystem. The results of our ongoing experiments with desert seed-eaters tend to support the conclusions outlined above. The absolute and relative abundances of both the remaining granivores and their food plants are altered substantially when seed-eating rodents are removed, but many of the responses (such as those of seed-eating birds) are compensatory so that they tend to preserve the homeostatic structure and function of the ecosystem as a whole.

This paper points out a lack of information about the ecological roles of vertebrates that is both distressing and encouraging. On the one hand, it is apparent that if we still know so little about the effects of the relatively few kinds of vertebrates on relatively simple desert ecosystems, it will be some time before we can hope to appreciate the impacts of the much more diverse vertebrate biotas on much more complex ecosystems such as tropical forests. On the other hand, owing in good part to research on desert organisms and their environments, some of the important questions and answers are beginning to emerge. Because of their inherent advantages for experimental field studies, I suspect that deserts will continue to serve as empirical models of how more complex ecosystems are organized and what functional roles their vertebrate inhabitants play in this organization.

ACKNOWLEDGMENTS

Numerous students and colleagues have spent time with me in the desert, assisted with field research, and shared ideas about the organization of desert ecosystems. Of these, R. M. Chew, D. W. Davidson, N. R. French, R. S. Inouye, Astrid Kodric-Brown, M. A. Mares, J. C. Munger,

O. J. Reichman, M. L. Rosenzweig, and W. G. Whitford deserve special mention. My research has been generously supported by my universities, by the Desert Biome, US/IBP, and by the National Science Foundation (most recently with Grant DEB 80–21535).

REFERENCES

Bennett, A. F., and W. R. Dawson. 1976. Metabolism, pp. 127–223. *In:* C. Gans and W. R. Dawson (eds.). The biology of the Reptilia, Vol. 5, Academic Press, New York.

Bennett, A. F., and K. A. Nagg. 1977. Energy expenditure of free-ranging lizards. Ecology 58:697–700.

Brown, J. H., and D. W. Davidson. 1977. Competition between seed-eating rodents and ants in desert ecosystems. Science 196:880–882.

Brown, J. H., D. W. Davidson, and O. J. Reichman. 1979. An experimental study of competition between seed-eating desert rodents and ants. American Zoologist 19:1115–1127.

Brown, J. H., O. J. Reichman, and D. W. Davidson. 1979. Granivory in desert ecosystems. Annual Review of Ecology and Systematics 10:201–227.

Bryant, M., D. J. DePree, S. Dick-Peddie, P. Hamilton, and W. G. Whitford. 1976. The impact of seed consumers in a desert ecosystem. US/IBP Desert Biome Research Memorandum 76–22:37–46.

Chew, R. M. 1974. Consumers as regulators of ecosystems: an alternative to energetics. Ohio Journal of Science 74:359–370.

Chew, R. M. and A. E. Chew. 1970. Energy relationships of the mammals of desert shrub (*Larrea tridentata*) community. Ecological Monographs 40:1–21.

Dunning, J. B., and J. H. Brown. 1982. Summer rainfall and winter sparrow densities: a test of the food limitation hypothesis. The Auk: 99:123–129.

Feder, M. E. 1976. Lunglessness, body size, and metabolic rate in salamanders. Physiological Zoology 49:398–406.

French, N. R., B. G. Maza, H. O. Hill, A. P. Aschwaden, and H. W. Kaaz. 1974. A population study of irradiated desert rodents. Ecological Monographs 44:45–72.

Golley, F. B. 1973. Impact of mammals on primary production, pp. 142–147. *In:* J. A. Gessaman (ed.). Ecological energetics of homeotherms. Utah State University Monograph Series, Vol. 20.

Grant, W. E., N. R. French, and L. J. Folse. 1980. Effects of pocket gopher mounds on plant production in shortgrass prairie ecosystems. Southwestern Naturalist 25:215–224.

Grinnell, J. 1923. The burrowing rodents of California as agents in soil formation. Journal of Mammalogy 4:137–149.

Humphreys, W. F. 1979. Production and respiration in animal populations. Journal of Animal Ecology 48:427–453.

Inouye, R. S. 1981. Interactions among unrelated species: granivorous rodents, a arasitic fungus, and a shared prey species. Oecologia 49:425–427.

Inouye, R. S. 1982. Population biology of desert annual plants. Ph.D. dissertation, University of Arizona.

Inouye, R. S., G. S. Byers, and J. H. Brown. 1980. Effect of predation and competition on survivorship, fecundity, and community structure of desert annuals. Ecology 61:1344–1351.

Martin, P. S., and H. E. Wright. 1967. Pleistocene extinctions. Yale University Press, New Haven, Conn.

McNeill, S., and J. H. Lawton. 1970. Annual production and respiration in animal populations. Nature 225:472–474.

Mielke, H. W. 1977. Mount building by pocket gophers (Geomyidae): their impact on soils and vegetation in North America. Journal of Biogeography 4:171–180.

Morton, S. R. 1979. Diversity of desert-dwelling mammals: a comparison of Australia and North America. Journal of Mammalogy 60:253–264.

Munger, J. C., and J. H. Brown. 1981. Competition in desert rodents: an experiment with semipermeable enclosures. Science 211:510–512.

Noy-Meir, I. 1973. Desert ecosystems: environment and producers. Annual Review of Ecology and Systematics 4:25–51.

Noy-Meir, I. 1974. Desert ecosystems: higher trophic levels. Annual Review of Ecology and Systematics 5:195–214.

Petrusewicz, K., F. B. Golley, and L. Ryszkowski (eds.). 1974. Productivity investigations of small mammals. Cambridge University Press, Cambridge, England.

Pianka, E. R. 1973. The structure of lizard communities. Annual Review of Ecology and Systematics 4:53–74.

Pyke, G. H., H. R. Pulliam, and E. L. Charnov. 1977. Optimal foraging: a selective review of theory and tests. The Quarterly Review of Biology 52:137–154.

Pough, F. H. 1980. The advantages of ectothermy for tetrapods. American Naturalist 415:92–112.

Pulliam, H. R., R. H. Parker. 1979. Population regulation of sparrows. Forschr. Zoology 25:137–147.

Raitt, R. J., and S. L. Pimm. 1976. Dynamics of bird communities in the Chihuahuan Desert, New Mexico. The Condor 78:427–492.

Steinberger, Y., and W. G. Whitford. 1983. The contribution of rodents to decomposition processes in a desert ecosystem. Journal of Arid Environments 6:177–181.

Steinberger, Y., and W. G. Whitford. 1983. The contribution of shrub pruning by jackrabbits to litter input in a Chihuahuan Desert ecosystem. Journal of Arid Environments 6:183–187.

Turner, F. B. 1970. The ecological efficiency of consumer populations. Ecology 51:741–742.

Whitford, W. G. 1976. Temporal fluctuation in density and diversity of desert rodent populations. Journal of Mammalogy 57:351–369.

4

THE ROLE OF INVERTEBRATES
IN DESERT ECOSYSTEMS

Clifford S. Crawford

The University of New Mexico
Albuquerque, New Mexico

INTRODUCTION

Processes underlying the dynamics of desert ecosystems reflect both the extremes of the physical environment and the paucity of available resources (see recent syntheses by Petrov 1976, Goodall and Perry 1979, 1981). These constraints directly or indirectly impinge on the life histories of all desert organisms, including invertebrates which are by far the most abundant animals in arid regions. While the general effects of the physical environment on desert invertebrates are reasonably clear (see reviews by Edney 1974, 1977, Cloudsley-Thompson 1975, Crawford 1981, Wallwork 1982), our knowledge of how these animals utilize available resources is less thorough. This is partly because spatial and temporal "patchiness" of nutritional resources in deserts—together with relatively stochastic arrival of moisture in arid regions—limit the accuracy with which we can predict foraging by individual species and feeding guilds. Further, foraging by desert invertebrates has received little rigorous attention, despite insightful observations made earlier by Buxton (1923), Andrewartha and Birch (1954), Cloudsley-Thompson and Chadwick (1964), and others. In the past decade, however, the association of desert invertebrate life history and environment, as well as the utilization of trophic resources by desert invertebrates, have come under increased scrutiny. Both approaches are needed if we are to understand the roles of invertebrates in arid ecosystems.

It is therefore relevant to ask whether such roles are played out in relative isolation—and consequently controlled largely by variations in the physical environment—or whether they are more likely to be elements of a complex network of biological feedbacks. Noy-Meir (1979–80) applied the question to desert organisms generally, and distinguished between an "autoecological hypothesis" (with few feedbacks) and the more conventional "ecosystem hypothesis" (with many feedbacks).

Here I deal with the same point by examining resource (largely food) utilization as it is influenced by *consumptive* and *life history processes*. To do this, I present a subjective overview of consumptive processes (herbivory, carnivory, and omnivory) as they relate to processes involving life history (reproduction, development, and behavior). Some of the consequences to desert ecosystems of the *functioning* of these processes are discussed simultaneously and are then brought together in a final synthesis.

I should emphasize that in this paper I apply the processes in question only to invertebrates, animals that on the whole are more efficient in growth but less eurythermal in activity than birds and mammals. Most invertebrates also are short-lived and therefore tend to develop quickly over brief spans of time. Parenthetically, if there is an apparent advantage to the rapid consumption of available energy and nutrients that attends accelerated development, it may be offset by the ecothermic constraint of restricted foraging duration, a problem also faced by amphibians and reptiles as well as by hibernating endotherms. Thus, consumer utilization of food resources in deserts can vary with and be dictated by alternative metabolic and life history strategies.

Regardless whether consumptive and life history processes contribute to isolated or to interconnected roles of desert invertebrates, they must still make some contribution to the dynamics of the environment in which these animals function. In this regard I assume that the relative *intensity* of process functioning (for example, rate of herbivory) can (1) control the level of resources on which invertebrate consumers depend, and (2) regulate rates of nutrient and energy flow in their habitats (see Chew 1974, for further discussion). If my assumptions are correct, then the extent to which either of these effects is manifested by a given species or guild should tell us much about the role of that trophic unit in its ecosystem.

In order to deal with the central question about roles of desert invertebrates, I find it convenient to frame three secondary questions and to organize the discussion that follows around them. The first of these asks whether there are characteristic *patterns* of process functioning among desert invertebrates. Actually, the bulk of the review focuses on this point and inevitably leads to the second question, which then asks what *ecological determinants* affect and control the expressions of the patterns. As we shall see, the determinants are factors with the potential to limit and thus regulate pattern expression. The third question asks what are the relative *impacts* on the ecosystem of patterns of process functioning. Looked at in the framework of energy and nutrient flow, impacts refer here to the controlling and regulating effects of process functioning; impacts are also summarized in remarks at the end of this paper.

PATTERNS OF PROCESS FUNCTIONING

I conceive of two types of process-functioning patterns that apply to desert invertebrates: *trophic-level* patterns characterizing consumptive processes, and *moisture-associated* patterns characterizing both consumptive and life history processes. I first examine a number of trophic-level patterns in regard to the availability and use of resources.

Trophic-Level Patterns

Patterns in the use of "nonreserve" plant biomass. "Nonreserve" plant biomass is considered here in the context of Noy-Meir's (1973) "pulse and reserve" model in which seeds and underground storage organs are termed *reserves*. Nonreserve material therefore applies to aboveground plant parts, including stems, leaves, fruits, and flowers, but, in the present paper, not to nectar and pollen, which I place in a separate category. For purposes of discussion, I divide the nonreserve category into perennial shrubs and ephemeral shoots.

Because of their relative longevities, perennial shrubs are usually conspicuous and reliable (that is, predictable) additions to desert landscapes. Flowering and leaf production in at least succulent and deep-rooted xerophyte shrubs seems generally independent of precipitation in deserts (Mooney et al. 1977, Solbrig et al. 1977). Arthropod consumers of this resource are relatively short-lived and include both generalists (polyphagous species) and specialists (oligophagous and monophagous species), with the latter group apparently dominating (Mann 1969, Orians et al. 1977, Cates 1981). Since specialists seem restricted to perennials with relatively rainfall-independent phenologies, it may be that most of these consumers are able to track their hosts by responding to the same cues (for example, temperature and day length) that promote leaf production, flowering, or fruiting.

In contrast, ephemeral shoots (annual forbs and grasses; geophytes) are on the whole less predictable in deserts. In fact, their seeds may remain viable for decennia (Went 1969), and depending on seed survival and germination their spatial distributions may vary greatly in a given habitat over time. However, by living as long or longer than ephemeral shoots, generalist foragers should be able to make effective use of such resources (Joern 1979). Evidence that they do so in deserts is given by Orians et al. (1977) and Cates (1981). Further, since the phenologies of many desert ephemerals are linked tightly to moisture (Ayyad 1981, Ludwig and Whitford 1981), the arrival of moisture should also be significant to the timing of development and activity of many generalist consumers.

How consistent is foraging pressure by arthropod consumers on desert nonreserve vegetation? The answer seems to depend in part on the relationship of plant type and environmental moisture. Short-lived, unpredictable plant hosts, on average, should be harder to find in relatively dry years than long-lived, predictable hosts. On the other hand, in "wet" years outbreaks of lepidopteran larvae, desert locusts, and other insects can locally decimate ephemeral hosts (references in Crawford 1981: 50, 211). Perennial plants, too, receive sporadic attacks by insect consumers (Larsen and Larsen 1980) that occasionally result in severe defoliation. In a review of the insects that feed on wild plants in long-disturbed Mediterranean desert ecosystems of northern Egypt, Moursi and Hegazi (1983) found that heavy infestations are not uncommon, particularly on flowers and fruits. Thus, while plant chemical defenses may operate effectively much of the time (Cates 1980), there are obvious exceptions to this situation, and it may be that in regions subject to long-term human disturbance, relatively fast growing plants such as *Asparagus* forbs do not possess the defenses of more persistent desert plants such as *Thymelaea* shrubs. An added variable about which little seems to be known in deserts is the growth-stimulating effect of phytophagy (Crawford 1981: 216). Until more evidence is in, I would agree with Noy-Meir (1979–81) that desert ephemerals—and I would include perennials as well—are not normally "limited" by at least aboveground invertebrate herbivores (but see further qualifying remarks under *Responses to aridity*, below).

Patterns of foraging for nectar and pollen. Many kinds of insects forage for nectar and pollen in deserts, where insect pollination is extremely important (Baker and Hurd 1968). Bees, wasps, and flies appear predominant, and a theoretical case has been made for the importance of ants as pollinators because of the presumed slight energetic cost of pollinating behavior to these social insects in a low-energy system (Hickman 1974). As it turns out, at least in the Americas, nonsocial bees do most of the pollinating in deserts (Linsley 1958). This may also have something to do with energy levels in deserts, for long-term nectar and pollen supplies may be insufficient to support colonies of social Hymenoptera in these places (Neff et al. 1977: 207), although Schaeffer et al. (1983) report that ants consume large quantities of agave nectar.

Specialist consumers of nectar and pollen, in deserts at least, operate under and respond to a somewhat different set of constraints compared to specialist consumers of other nonreserve plant material. For example, many oligolectic North American nonsocial desert bees (those having few host species) utilize the blooms of annual plants, and even the relatively unpredictable blooms of perennials such as *Larrea* spp. (Simpson et al. 1977a). Many oligolectic species also visit more predictable perennial blooms (Simpson et al. 1977b). Therefore, predictability of the resource in question may be relatively unimportant in determining the foraging patterns of these specialist consumers in deserts. Instead, because temporal, mechanical, and spatial displacements are common among both oligoletic and polyletic desert bees (Simpson et al. 1977b), resource partitioning *during* bloom may be of enhanced significance.

Foraging displacements may be related to actual or potential competition (Simpson et al. 1977a,b), and to timing of floral traits such as opening and closing (Linsley 1978). Thus, small-bodied *Perdita* bees are specialists that tend to visit all anthers on *Prosopis* flowers during the heat of the day, while large-bodied, often polylectic bees generally fly early in the day (and season) and visit only those flowers where resources are highly available (Simpson et al. 1978b). Such evidence suggests that pollen and nectar are limiting to insect consumers in deserts and that intense species interactions characterize foraging for these resources.

Patterns in the use of "reserve" plant biomass. Considering the immense amount of underground plant biomass in deserts (Ludwig 1977), it is unfortunate that so little is known of its use by invertebrate consumers. Nematodes, cockroaches, cicadas, and the larvae of coleopterans, lepidopterans, and dipterans have been reported as root or tuber foragers feeding on native desert vegetation (Crawford 1981); however, the extent of this kind of foraging is difficult to assess comprehensively.

Seed consumption by desert invertebrates, especially ants, has been studied more intensely. Other insects (for example, bruchid coleopterans, which may damage most of the seeds of Negev desert acacias [Shalmon 1982]) also consume seeds of desert plants, but granivorous ants are clearly the major species in this guild. And, as in the case of nectar-pollen foragers, many of these insects are specialists—albeit opportunistic foragers (see below). This suggests the importance of competition for a sometimes limited resource, with the abundance of seeds in deserts being highly variable in space and time (Went and Westergaard 1949). However, unlike pollen and nectar, seeds last a long time and therefore present a potentially great amount of biomass to consumers.

Specialization by granivorous ants is evident in certain of their morphological, physiological, and behavioral traits. Size differences within the harvester guild are, for example, associated with the sizes of seeds taken (references in Brown et al. 1979, Crawford 1981: 161–162; see also Melhop and Scott 1983). Differences in desiccation-resistance may also be related to temporal differences in the diel activity of *Pogonomyrmex* species (Hansen 1978).

Foraging patterns are complex in desert harvesters. Davidson (1977) showed that some species are primarily group foragers (exploiting high density seed sources), while others tend to be individual foragers (exploiting dispersed seed sources). Intraspecific flexibility is seen also in the foraging behavior of some harvesters, with individual foraging being generally diurnal and group foraging capable of shifting to crepuscular and nocturnal hours (references in Brown et al. 1979). Moreover, foraging intensity in some species is related to seed abundance in a given year as well as to seed species and availability (Ben Mordechai and Kugler 1978, Whitford 1978).

There is indirect evidence that seeds are limiting to granivore ants. Colonies, for instance, are sometimes overdispersed (Briese and Macauley 1977), implying interference competition for a limited resource. Then, too, colony density may vary with primary productivity (Sneva 1979). In addition, some species forage at higher than normal ambient temperatures when offered special bait (Wisdom and Whitford 1981). Finally, it is likely that desert ants and rodents compete for seeds (Brown and Davidson 1977, Davidson et al. 1980).

Seed predation by desert ants can be extensive, with certain seeds being sometimes nearly completely harvested in an area (Whitford 1978). Also, exclusion of harvester species from experimental plots can significantly increase the seed densities of some plant species (Brown et al. 1979). On the other hand, dispersal of *Acacia* seeds by ants (and birds) in arid Australia directs these propagules to microhabitats potentially favorable to germination (Davidson and Morton 1984). Thus, while the seed-granivore system in deserts may be mutually limiting and characterized by feedback effects, as Noy-Meir (1979–80) has suggested, it contains complexities that defy simple modeling.

Patterns of carnivory.   Given the constraints of desert climates, vertebrate predators, and unevenly dispersed prey, it may be that foraging effort by invertebrate carnivores generally is geared to coincide with prey availability. This interpretation seems to hold for the scorpion *Paruroctonus mesaensis* (Polis 1980a), but not for its congener *P. utahensis* (Bradley 1983). The association may also be surmised for *Dinothrombium* mites, which emerge briefly after rains that trigger a simultaneous emergence of termite prey (Tevis and Newell 1962). Foraging according to prey availability probably applies as well to some desert spiders (Reichert 1978, Kronk and Reichert 1979), and may be inferred for whipscorpions and scolopendromorph centipedes (Crawford 1981). Most of these relatively large-bodied and generally nocturnal species undergo what I term *flexible quiescence*, for when they are not foraging they can remain for long periods in burrows or in other protected habitats. Relatively low metabolic rates, coupled with a pronounced ability to starve, contribute effectively to this state of temporary dormancy (see the discussion in Crawford 1981: chap. 11).

Although there are some conspicuous exceptions—for example, ant-eating trapdoor spiders (Main 1957)—most of the larger invertebrate carnivores in deserts seem to be general feeders, but unlike many vertebrate carnivores in deserts (Noy-Meir 1974, Reichmann et al. 1979) their diet does not include plants.

A number of studies suggest that invertebrate carnivores in arid regions make optimal use of foraging space and/or minimal use of foraging time. The first of these paradigms is supported by or inferred from demonstrations of fitness reduction in crowded *Agelinopsis* spiders (Reichert 1978), regular spacing of *Myrmeleon* ant lion pits (McClure 1976), and by extensive cannibalism in a *Parurocturus* scorpion (Polis 1980b). These examples imply interference competition. Hunting-time minimization is also documented, particularly for large spiders (Shook 1978) and scorpions (Hadley and Williams 1968, Bradley,, 1983). These arachnids forage at night in small numbers relative to their population sizes, and capture prey at remarkably low rates.

Out of ignorance I have omitted consideration of virtually all small-bodied, soil-bound species, such as predaceous nematodes, mites, and insect larvae. Nevertheless, observations on the larger-bodied groups, mentioned above (also, see Louw and Seely 1982: 132), lead me to several thoughts that may apply generally to desert invertebrate carnivores. First, the actual feeding of these organisms may be restricted by predator pressure (large invertebrates in particular may be easy for vertebrate carnivores to spot) and limited feeding opportunities. Second, invertebrate carnivores probably seldom impact severely on populations of their desert prey.

Patterns of omnivory.   Invertebrates that normally ingest detritus but that occasionally eat living organisms are extremely common in deserts. Although the term *omnivore* correctly applies to many of these species, *detritivore* is equally if not more appropriate because of its trophic emphasis and previous usage (Crawford 1979). It should be noted that detritus, largely in the form of plant litter, can accumulate in large quantities in deserts—perhaps because of slow rates of decomposition (Seely and Luow 1980, West 1979; but also see Whitford herein). Thus, a considerable quantity of irregularly distributed nutrition that may also act as a habitat matrix is available to many desert invertebrates.

Foraging by desert detritivores should be strongly conditioned by climate and perhaps less directly by food availability and quality. This statement is based on three related notions. First, there is good evidence that assemblages of small-bodied, usually short-lived invertebrates in the decomposer complex of desert soil and litter require moisture for appreciable activity. This is certainly true for many nematodes (Freckman 1978) and microarthropods (Whitford et al. 1981) and, by inference from anecdotal information and many observations, for larvae of many holometabolous insects as well. Further, termite activity such as spreading carton over consumable surface objects, and also producing alates, can also be promoted by seasonal moisture (see the references in Crawford 1981). However, while the life cycle of *Hemilepistus* isopods is in some ways linked to rainfall in the Negev desert, the foraging of these desert crustaceans also occurs during dry seasons when soil and litter are moistened by fog or dew (Shachak et al. 1976).

Second, climatic conditioning of foraging also holds for certain large-bodied, long-lived taxa, including gastropod mollusks and millipedes (Crawford 1979). As might be expected, their foraging dependence on atmospheric moisture is not necessarily direct; some desert snails seldom forage when the surface is dry (Shachak et al. 1975, Steinberger et al. 1981), while some desert millipedes display comparatively flexible patterns of seasonal foraging regardless of surface moisture (Crawford and Warburg 1982).

Third, the absolute abundance of food may have little to do with its real availability to consumers. This idea is derived from the two given above, and implies the obvious, namely, that while they are inactive detritivores do not feed appreciably (although they may be processing previously ingested food; see below).

As to whether or not the quality of detritus relates to its consumption in deserts, many unpublished field observations and examinations of gut contents of spirostreptid millipedes and tenebrionid beetles (larvae and adults) suggest to me that foraging per se by such animals is geared to food availability in the habitat but that is is otherwise not particularly selective. However, Rogers et al. (1978) found that food plant species selection does differ among different groups of these beetles in shrub-steppe communities of southcentral Washington. A wide assortment of plant material, organic debris, fungi, and mineral matter is found in the guts of desert detritivores. Yet detritus quality, in the sense of litter hydration (Tschinkel 1972), topographic variation of fungi (Taylor 1979), and presence of recalcitrant compounds (Shaefer and Whitford 1981) may influence detritivore feeding. Taylor (1982a) has shown that desert millipedes prefer some fungal species over others. The food-niche breadth of desert detritus feeders offers a rich field for study.

A largely overlooked aspect of the role of desert detritivores concerns the contribution to decomposition of ingested materials by gut symbionts. The capacity of some of these microorganisms to fix nitrogen is addressed in this volume by Whitford (also, see Crawford 1979) and will not be dealt with further here. Other ingested microbes promote nitrogen mineralization or cellulose decomposition following defecation by desert cockroaches and tenebrionids, respectively, on external substrates (El-Ayouty et al. 1978, Mordkovich and Afanes'ev 1980). Such roles may be very significant to localized decomposition.

Another major contribution of gut microbes may be that of *in situ* cellulose breakdown. Taylor (1982b) has shown that as a consequence of experimentally reduced gut floras there is a reduction of cellulose degradation and assimilation in host desert millipedes. Taylor and Crawford (1982) reasoned that, because of prolonged collective seasonal activity in the desert detritivore community, cellulolytic gut microbes may allow a fairly continuous cellulose breakdown in spite of conditions in the external environment that should frequently inhibit free-living microbes. Support for this view has been documented with detritivores inhabiting a small dune system in New Mexico (Crawford and Taylor 1984).

Moisture-associated Patterns

Moisture-associated patterns of process functioning, for purposes of this discussion, apply to both the consumptive processes outlined in the previous section and to life history processes such as reproduction, development and behavior. I now divide moisture-associated patterns into two overlapping categories: responses to moisture and responses to aridity.

Responses to moisture. The concept of longevity provides a useful framework for a description of responses to moisture. Accordingly, I distinguish between the responses of two life history groups of desert invertebrates. The first consists of short-lived and/or primary consumers (especially those found on ephemeral vegetation) having life cycles closely tied to moisture events.

What is known or can be inferred about their life histories suggests that many of these species fit the classical "r-selected" scheme. These taxa include free-living soil nematodes and microarthropods (except for long-lived cryptostigmatid mites), and probably most primary consumer insects as well. It is hardly surprising that the presence or arrival of moisture should have profound effects on the activity and population levels of such organisms in otherwise dry environments (Cloudsley-Thompson and Idris 1964). Indeed, the same pulses of incoming precipitation that "drive" primary production (Noy-Meir 1974) may be more important than changes in day length or temperature to synchronous activity in this desert assemblage.

The second moisture-response group includes comparatively long-lived species belonging to all major trophic levels. While precipitation clearly exerts some influence on the life histories of these species, its effect may be secondary or indirect relative to other factors. Examples come from such unrelated taxa as *Pyrota* meloid coleopterans that as adults emerge synchronously with the flowering of mesquite trees (Mathieu 1980), from *Paruroctonus* scorpions that appear on the surface of North American deserts at times unrelated to precipitation (inferred from Polis 1980; see also, observations by R. A. Bradley, W. A. Riddle, and myself), and from *Orthoporus* millipedes that molt synchronously belowground in the southwestern United States prior to the onset of summer rains (Crawford 1981). These few examples suggest that among long-lived desert invertebrates proximal responses to moisture are of less relevance than general developmental strategies attuned to a variety of stimuli.

Responses to aridity.   Three rather unrelated patterns of response to aridity come to mind in regard to roles of invertebrates in desert ecosystems. One pattern concerns faunal activity relative to seasonal drought. With the exception of Péfaur's (1981) study in the Peruvian coastal desert, gross faunal changes with season have seldom been measured rigorously in arid regions. Nevertheless, the small amount of evidence available suggests that invertebrate populations should generally exhibit peak activities (also read "consumption") *early* in the "dry" seasons of arid regions. Obviously there are many qualifiers to such a prediction, not the least of which is that there may be more than one dry season per year in a given desert. Also, in some deserts drought is essentially aseasonal. Further, drought may occur in winter or in summer, depending on the desert. Still, one can reason that following a wet season the subsequent waves of primary production (Ludwig and Whitford 1981: 294) and attendant consumption (Paramanov, 1959: 183) should last for some time. Pietruska's (1980) study in the Great Basin desert showed that densities of total surface and aerial arthropods peaked about 1.5 months following spring rains. Péfaur (1981) actually determined a dramatic rise in invertebrate density toward the end of the wet season in Peru, and species there remained abundant early in the subsequent dry season.

Another feature of peak activity early in seasonal drought involves trophic level. Looking only at herbivory, I would expect a major trophic-level consequence of the presumed activity peak in early dry season consumption (see above) to be increased grazing pressure by generalist consumers on nonreserve biomass—at a time when plants begin to undergo increased moisture stress. If so, then there may be unusual seasons or years in a desert when arthropods consuming aboveground plant parts have important limiting effects on their food resources. Feedback of this sort accords with my earlier conclusion that invertebrate herbivory in deserts should not *normally* limit primary producers.

A second pattern of response to aridity is taken in part from arguments advanced by Remmert (1981), suggesting that a relative increase in body size may accompany aridity and that sociality may be favored also in arid environments. These ideas are based largely on extensive arthropod collections over a broad geographic moisture gradient. They are of interest here because they touch on several points made earlier in this paper.

An increase in arthropod body size with aridity was felt by Reimmert (1981) to have been selected because of the accompanying decreased risk of desiccation. I would argue further that since large size often correlates with long life in desert invertebrates, and because many long-lived species are either detritivores or carnivores, a relative size increase should have trophic implications. It is interesting that detritivores (including harvester ants) in the Egyptian coastal desert do, in fact, achieve the greatest biomass (and density) among soil mesofauna (Ghabbour and Shakir 1980).

Remmert (1981) also predicted that predators of insects in dry biotopes should be comparatively large in body size. To this, I would add that an increased density of arthropod carnivores (preying mainly on insects) with aridity is moderately well supported from results of several studies. Péfaur (1981) found that faunas (including some vertebrates) are mainly carnivorous at xeric low elevations in the Peruvian coastal desert, but may be predominantly herbivorous at higher elevations where primary production is greater. Seely and Louw (1980) considered the proportion of carnivores to herbivores and omnivores (1:7.4—wet weight—some vertebrates included) in the Namib desert to be relatively high. Ghabbour and Shakir's (1982) ratio for *invertebrate* mesofauna in Egypt (recalculated by me) comes to 1:16.5, while Chew's (1981) ratio for spider predators to insect prey in a desert shrub community is 1:3.5. In addition, data from several authors cited by Crawford (1981: 153–155) give roughly similar ratios for desert soil mites, among which predaceous species may make a disproportionately high contribution to energy flow. Wagner and Graetz (1981) compared percentages of predatory faunas in deserts with those from mesic regions and found the former generally to be higher. Indeed, if carnivores (among invertebrates for our purposes) are relatively more abundant in deserts than elsewhere, and if a classical predator–prey lag applies to these species and to their food, the effect may be to damp the presumed occasional limiting influence of generalist herbivores on above-ground vegetation in early drought (see above).

The third pattern of response stems from Remmert's (1981) prediction that arthropod sociality may be favored by aridity, a prediction based on the assumption that an increase in arthropod parental care occurs in arid regions. Does the evidence support this idea? To some extent I feel that it does. As Remmert points out, the only known social isopods (mainly detritivores) occur in deserts. And while the actual numbers of ant and termite species in deserts are not particularly high, these are often hugely abundant organisms with tremendous potential for moving energy and nutrients in deserts (Crawford 1981). Moreover, they forage on resources (for example, seeds, detritus) that should normally supply colony needs in a sustained manner. The relationship is quite unlike that existing between social bees and their floral resources (see above) and that known for social spiders (not found in typical desert situations) and their abundant prey (Riechert 1978). Therefore sociality may have been selected in deserts for reasons associated with juvenile survival and colony maintenance in instances where energy demands were below a certain threshold.

SOME GENERAL CONCLUSIONS

Initially I posed three secondary questions relating to the roles of invertebrates in desert ecosystems. Now I shall attempt to provide some answers, each being based on the discussion embodied in the previous section.

The first question asked whether characteristic patterns of process functioning exist among desert invertebrates. The simple answer is that both consumptive and life history processes do indeed seem to show characteristic patterns at all trophic levels. These are patterns, moreover, that reflect the spatial and temporal distribution of patchy nutritional resources. Briefly now—and for the moment declining to comment on the impacts of patterns of process functioning in deserts—let me summarize what I consider to be the essential features of each consumptive pattern among desert invertebrates.

1. Consumers of nonreserve vegetation tend to be specialists when their host plants are relatively predictable resources, and to be generalists when host plants are ephemeral shoots.

2. Consumers (both generalists and specialists) of nectar and pollen rely strongly on spatial and/or temporal partitioning of host resources, but perhaps less on the predictability of those resources.

3. Consumers (especially seed-harvesting ants) of reserve vegetation also partition host resources; mechanisms for doing so are frequently associated with sociality but are not necessarily associated with resource predictability.

4. Carnivores tend to rely on combinations of space optimizing—that reduces interference competition—and time minimizing—that avoids predator pressure and allows effective use of available prey.

5. Omnivores (mainly detritivores) are, in general, highly responsive to climate; however, because of their gut symbionts they are capable of processing ingested materials even when climate precludes active foraging.

The second question asked what ecological determinants control the expressions of these patterns. The main determinants seem evident enough: nutrients (including usable energy), water, and aspects of the physical and biotic environment (such as temperature extremes and soil texture) that affect invertebrate activity and distribution. While constraints controlling consumption have been emphasized in this paper, the entire spectrum of determinants can be treated collectively as operating in a fairly stochastic manner in space and time. Thus, whether determinants are resources that promote fitness or agencies that reduce fitness, their operation in deserts is characterized by varying levels of uncertainty. Predicting the effects of invertebrate roles in arid regions clearly cannot be accomplished at high levels of resolution from short-term studies.

The third question asked what are the relative impacts of patterns of process functioning on nutrient and energy flow in deserts. If we acknowledge the importance of incoming moisture pulses—in terms of their direct or indirect influence on invertebrate regulation of nutrient and energy flows through trophic levels—then we need to ascertain when and where the greatest regulation takes place. This requires that we focus once again on the consumers themselves, and leads us to two general predictions.

The first prediction is that the relative uncertainty of incoming moisture in deserts should usually have a *direct, short-term* effect on consumers of nonreserve ephemeral vegetation, and on the foraging of many small-bodied species (that is, many nematodes, microarthropods, and insects). These animals—deep-soil inhabitants excepted—should be the first to feel the effects of drought, either via their food or through desiccation stress.

In contrast, we may predict that incoming moisture should usually have a more *indirect, long-term* effect on consumers of nectar and pollen, on large carnivores, on large omnivores (detritivores), and on consumers of nonreserve plant biomass. Placement of nectar-pollen feeders in this category is an arguable point; I have done so on the assumption that most nonsocial specialist bees have enough temporal flexibility built into their life cycles to cope with erratic germination of their often ephemeral resources. Large invertebrate carnivores and omnivores in deserts appear able to go without feeding for long periods; the extent to which their life histories depend on moisture cues to trigger both consumptive and nonconsumptive processes varies, of course, with the species. Seed and belowground foragers on plant material generally occupy habitats where low moisture levels ought not to be a significant mortality factor.

As a consequence of these predicted relationships to incoming moisture, and in the light of comments given earlier in this text, it should be possible to relate consumer-resource interactions to the question of impacts. At any rate, I shall try to do so in the following concluding remarks.

Except for years or seasons when carnivores and consumers of nonreserve vegetation are unusually abundant (the latter early in the dry season), I would expect relatively little feedback by these animals on their resources. Alternatively, evidence cited above suggests that detritivores and consumers of reserve plant biomass can greatly increase the rates at which their nutritional resources disappear. This may be true for nectar-pollen feeders as well, assuming that declining populations have adverse effects on the seed set of host plants. In general, therefore, the last three groups should have the greatest direct impact on energy and nutrient flow in deserts. Finally, we should note that all three are strongly soil-associated, which is a fitting observation since it reinforces the status of soil as the primary matrix within and on which large-scale invertebrate roles in deserts are played.

ACKNOWLEDGMENTS

Ideas developed in this paper owe much to the insightful comments and reports of many colleagues. I thank Harvey Alexander, Rex Cates, and Rich Bradley for useful criticisms of an earlier draft.

REFERENCES

Andrewartha, H. C., and L. C. Birch. 1954. The distribution and abundance of animals. University of Chicago Press, Chicago, London.

Ayyad, M. A. 1981. Soil-vegetation-atmosphere interactions, pp. 9–13. *In:* D. W. Goodall, and R. A. Perry (eds.). Arid-land ecosystems: Structure, functioning and management. Vol. 2. IBP No. 17, Cambridge University Press, Cambridge, London, New York, New Rochelle, Melbourne, Sydney.

Baker, H. G., and P. D. Hurd, Jr. 1968. Intrafloral ecology. Annual Review of Entomology 13:385–414.

Bradley, R. A. 1983. Activity and population dynamics of the desert grassland scorpion (*Paruroctonus utahensis*): Does adaptation imply optimization? Ph.D. dissertation, University of New Mexico.

Ben Mordechai, Y., and J. Kugler. 1978. The adaptation of the food collecting seasons and the occurrence of the nuptial flight of ants to the ecological conditions in the desert loess plain of Sde Boqer (Sde-Zin). Page 6. Abstract, Fourth International Congress of Ecology, Jerusalem.

Briese, D. T., and B. J. Macauley. 1977. Physical structure of an ant community in semi-arid Australia. Australian Journal of Ecology 2:107–120.

Brown, J. H., and D. W. Davidson. 1977. Competition between seed-eating rodents and ants in desert ecosystems. Science 196:880–882.

Brown, J. H., Reichman, O. J. and D. W. Davidson. 1979. Granivory in desert ecosystems. Annual Review of Ecology and Systematics 10:201–227.

Buxton, P. A. 1923. Animal life in deserts—A study of fauna in relation to environment. Edward Arnold and Company, London.

Cates, R. G. 1980. Feeding patterns of monophagous, oligophagous, and polyphagous insect herbivores: The effects of resource abundance and plant chemistry. Oecologia 46:22–31.

Cates, R. G. 1981. Host plant predictability and the feeding patterns of monophagous, oligophagous, and polyphagous insect herbivores. Oecologia 48:319–326.

Chew, R. M. 1961. Ecology of spiders of a desert community. Journal of the New York Entomological Society 69:5–41.

Chew, R. M. 1974. Consumers as regulators of ecosystems: An alternative to energetics. Ohio Journal of Science 74:359–370.

Cloudsley-Thompson, J. L. 1975. Adaptations of Arthropoda to arid environments. Annual Review of Entomology 20:261–283.

Cloudsley-Thompson, J. L., and M. J. Chadwick. 1964. Life in deserts. Dufour Editions, Philadelphia.

Cloudsley-Thompson, J. L., and B. E. M. Idris. 1964. The insect fauna of the desert near Khartoum: Seasonal fluctuation and the effect of grazing. Proceedings of the Royal Entomological Society of London, Series A, 39:41–46.

Crawford, C. S. 1979. Desert detritivores: a review of life history patterns and trophic rôles. Journal of Arid Environments 2:31–42.

Crawford, C. S. 1981. Biology of desert invertebrates. Springer-Verlag, Berlin, Heidelberg, New York.

Crawford, C. S., and M. R. Warburg. Water balance and apparent oocyte resorption in desert millipedes. Journal of Experimental Zoology 222:215–226.

Crawford, C. S., and E. C. Taylor. 1984. Decomposition in arid environments: Role of the detritivore gut. South African Journal of Science 80:170–176.

Davidson, D. W. 1977. Foraging ecology and community organization in desert seed-eating ants. Ecology 58:711–724.

Davidson, D. W., J. H. Brown, and R. S. Inoye. 1980. Competition and the structure of granivore communities. BioScience 30:233–238.

Edney, E. B. 1974. Desert arthropods, pp. 311–384. *In:* G. W. Brown, Jr. (ed.). Desert biology. Vol. 2. Academic Press, London, New York.

Edney, E. B. 1977. Water balance in land arthropods. Springer-Verlag, Berlin, Heidelberg, New York.

El-Ayouty, E. Y., S. I. Ghabbour, and N. A. M. El-Sayyed. 1978. Role of litter and the excreta of desert fauna in the nitrogen status of desert soils. Journal of Arid Environments 1:145–155.

Freckman, D. W. 1978. Ecology of anhydrobiotic soil nematodes, pp. 345–357. *In:* J. H. Crowe, and J. S. Clegg (eds.). Dried biological systems. Academic Press, London, New York.

Ghabbour, S. I., and S. H. Shakir. 1980. Ecology of soil fauna in Mediterranean desert ecosystems in Egypt. III—Analysis of *Thymelea* mesofauna populations at the Maeiut frontal plain. Revue Écologie de Sol 17:327–352.

Goodall, D. W., and R. A. Perry (eds.). 1979. Arid-land ecosystems: Structures, functioning and management. Vol. 1. IBP No. 16, Cambridge University Press, Cambridge, New York, London, Melbourne.

Goodall, D. W., and R. A. Perry (eds.). 1981. Arid-land ecosystems: Structure, functioning and management. Vol. 2. IBP No. 17, Cambridge University Press, Cambridge, New York, New Rochelle, London, Melbourne, Sydney.

Hadley, N. F., and S. C. Williams. 1968. Surface activities of some North American scorpions in relation to feeding. Ecology 49:726–734.

Hansen, S. R. 1978. Resource utilization and coexistence of three species of *Pogonomyrmex* ants in the Upper Sonoran Grassland Community. Oecologia 35:190–117.

Hickman, J. C. 1974. Pollination by ants: A low-energy system. Science 184:1290–1292.

Joern, A. Feeding patterns in grasshoppers (Orthoptera: Acrididae): Factors influencing diet specialization. Oecologia 38:324–347.

Kronk, A. E., and S. E. Riechert. 1979. Parameters affecting the habitat choice of a desert wolf spider *Lycosa santrita* Chamberlin and Ivie. Journal of Arachnology 7:155–166.

Larsen, T., and K. Larsen. 1980. Butterflies of Oman. John Bartholomew and Sons, Edinburgh.

Linsley, E. G. 1958. The ecology of solitary bees. Hilgardia 27:543–599.

Linsley, E. G. 1978. Temporal patterns of flower visitation by solitary bees, with particular reference to the southwestern United States. Journal of the Kansas Entomological Society 51:531–546.

Louw, G. N., and M. K. Seely. 1982. Ecology of desert organisms. Longman, London and New York.

Ludwig, J. A. 1977. Distributional adaptations of root-systems in desert environments, pp. 85–91. *In:* E. K. Marshall (ed.). The belowground symposium: A synthesis of plant-associated processes. Range Science Department, Science Series No. 26, Colorado State University, Fort Collins.

Ludwig, J. A., and W. G. Whitford. 1981. Short-term water and energy flow in desert ecosystems, pp. 271–299. *In:* D. W. Goodall and R. A. Perry (eds.). Arid-land ecosystems, structure, functioning and management. Vol. 2. IBP No. 17, Cambridge University Press, Cambridge, London, New York, New Rochelle, Melbourne, Sydney.

Main, B. Y. 1957. Biology of aganippine trapdoor spiders (Mygalomorphae: Ctenizidae). Australian Journal of Zoology 5:402–473.

Mann, J. 1969. Cactus-feeding insects and mites. Smithsonian Institution, U.S. National Museum Bulletin No. 256.

Mathieu, J. M. 1980. The ontogeny of blister beetles (Coleoptera, Meloidae) IV.—*Pyrota insulata* Leconte. Southwest Naturalist 5:149–152.

McClure, M. S. 1976. Spatial distribution of pit-making ant lion larvae (Neuroptera: Myrmeleontidae): density effects. Biotropica 8:179–183.

Melhop, P., and N. J. Scott. 1983. Temporal patterns of seed use and availability in a guild of desert ants. Ecological Entomology 8:69–85.

Mooney, H. A., B. B. Simpson, and O. T. Solbrig. 1977. Phenology, morphology, physiology, pp. 26–43. *In:* B. B. Simpson (ed.). Mesquite—Its biology in two desert ecosystems. US/IBP Synthesis Series No. 4. Dowden, Hutchinson and Ross, Stroudsburg, Pennsylvania.

Mordkovich, V. G., and N. A. Afanas'ev. 1980. Transformation of steppe litter by darkling beetles. Ekologiya No. 3:56–62.

Moursi, K. S., and E. M. Hegazi. 1983. Destructive insects of wild plants in the Egyptian Western Desert. Journal of Arid Environments 6:119–127.

Neff, J. L., B. B. Simpson, and A. R. Moldenke. 1977. Flowers-flower visitor system, pp. 204–224. *In:* G. H. Orians and O. T. Solbrig (eds.). Convergent evolution in warm deserts. US/IBP Synthesis Series 3. Dowden, Hutchinson and Ross, Stroudsburg, Pennsylvania.

Noy-Meir, I. 1973. Desert ecosystems: Environment and producers. Annual Review of Ecology and Systematics 4:25–51.

Noy-Meir, I. 1974. Desert ecosystems: Higher trophic levels. Annual Review of Ecology and Systematics 5:195–213.

Noy-Meir, I. 1979/80. Structure and function of desert ecosystems. Israel Journal of Botany 28:1–19.

Orians, G. H., R. G. Cates, M. A. Mares, A. Moldenke, J. Neff, D. F. Rhoades, M. L. Rosenzweig, B. B. Simpson, J. C. Schultz, and C. S. Tomoff. 1977. Resource utilization systems, pp. 164–224. *In:* G. H. Orians and O. T. Solbrig (eds.). Convergent evolution in warm deserts. US/IBP Synthesis Series No. 3. Dowden, Hutchinson and Ross, Stroudsburg, Pennsylvania.

Paramonov, S. J. 1959. Zoogeographical aspects of the Australian dipterofauna, pp. 164–191. *In:* A. Keast, R. L. Crocker, and C. S. Christian (eds.). Biogeography and ecology in Australia. Dr. Junk Publishers. The Hague.

Péfaur, J. E. 1981. Composition and phenology of epigeic animal communities in the Lomas of southern Peru. Journal of Arid Environments 4:31–42.

Petrov, M. P. 1976. Deserts of the world. John Wiley and Sons, New York, Toronto.

Pietruszka, R. D. 1980. Observations on seasonal variation in desert arthropods in central Nevada. Great Basin Naturalist 40:292–297.

Polis, G. A. 1980a. Seasonal patterns and age-specific variation in the surface activity of a population of desert scorpions in relation to environmental factors. Journal of Animal Ecology 49:1–18.

Polis, G. A. 1980b. The effect of cannibalism on the demography and activity of a natural population of desert scorpions. Behavioral and Ecological Sociobiology 7:25–35.

Reichman, O. J., I. Prakash, and V. Roig. 1979. Food selection and consumption, pp. 681–716. *In:* D. W. Goodall and R. A. Perry (eds.). Arid-land ecosystems: Structure, functioning and management. IBP No. 16, Cambridge University Press, Cambridge, London, New York, Melbourne.

Remmert, H. 1981. Body size of terrestrial arthropods and biomass of their populations in relation to the abiotic parameters of their milieu. Oecologia 50:12–13.

Riechert, S. E. 1978. Energy-based territoriality in populations of the desert spider *Agelenopsis aperta* (Gertsch). Symposium of the Zoological Society of London No. 42:211–222.

Rogers, L. E., N. Woodley, J. K. Sheldon, and V. A. Uresk. 1976. Darkling beetle populations (Tenebrionidae) of the Hanford Site in Southcentral Washington. Research Report PNL–2465/UC–11, Battelle, Pacific Northwest Laboratories.

Schaefer, D. A., and W. G. Whitford. 1981. Nutrient cycling by the subterranean termite *Gnathamitermes tubiformans* in a Chihuahuan desert ecosystem. Oecologia 48:277–283.

Schaeffer, W. M., D. W. Zeh, S. L. Buchmann, S. Kleinhans, M. V. Schaeffer, and J. Antrim. 1983. Competition for nectar between introduced honey bees and native North American bees and ants. Ecology 64:564–577.

Seely, M. K., and G. N. Louw. 1980. First approximation of the effects of rainfall on the ecology and energetics of a Namib Desert dune ecosystem. Journal of Arid Environments 3:25–54.

Shachak, M., E. A. Chapman, and Y. Steinberger. 1976. Feeding, energy flow and soil turnover in the desert isopod, *Hemilepistus reaumuri*. Oecologia 24:57–69.

Shachak, M., Y. Orr, and Y. Steinberger. 1975. Field observations on the natural history of *Sphincterochila (S.) zonata* (Bourguignat, 1853) (= *S. boissieri* Charpentier, 1847). Argamon. Israel Journal of Malacology 5:20–46.

Shalmon, B. 1982. Miniature tropical world among acacias. Israel—Land and Nature 7:152–161.

Shook, R. S. 1978. Ecology of the wolf spider *Lycosa carolinensis* Walkenauer (Araneae: Lycosidae) in a desert community. Journal of Arachnology 6:53–64.

Simpson, B. B., J. L. Neff, and A. R. Moldenke. 1977a. Reproductive systems of *Larrea*, pp. 92–114. *In:* T. J. Mabry, J. H. Hunziker, and D. R. Difeo, Jr. (eds.). Creosote bush—Biology and chemistry of *Larrea* in New World deserts. US/IBP Synthesis Series 6. Dowden, Hutchinson and Ross, Stroudsburg, Pennsylvania.

Simpson, B. B., J. L. Neff, and A. R. Moldenke. 1977b. *Prosopis* flowers as a resource, pp. 84–107. *In:* B. B. Simpson (ed.). Mesquite—Its biology in two desert scrub ecosystems. US/IBP Synthesis Series 4. Dowden, Hutchinson and Ross, Stroudsburg, Pennsylvania.

Sneva, F. A. 1979. The western harvester ants: Their density and hill size in relation to herbaceous productivity and big sagebrush cover. Journal of Range Management 32:46–47.

Solbrig, O. T., M. A. Barbour, J. Cross, G. Goldstein, C. H. Lowe, J. Morello, and T. W. Yang. 1977. The strategies and community patterns of desert plants, pp. 68–106. *In:* G. H. Orians, and O. T. Solbrig (eds.). Convergent evolution in warm deserts. US/IBP Synthesis Series No. 3. Dowden, Hutchinson and Ross, Stroudsburg, Pennsylvania.

Steinberger, Y., S. Grossman, and Z. Dubinsky. 1981. Some aspects of the ecology of the desert snail *Sphincterochila prophetarum* in relation to energy and water flow. Oecologia 50:103–108.

Taylor, E. C. 1979. Seasonal distribution and abundance of fungi in two desert grassland communities. Journal of Arid Environments 2:295–312.

Taylor, E. C. 1982a. Fungal preference by *Orthoporus ornatus* (Girard: Spirostreptidae), a desert millipede. Pedobiologia 23:331–336.

Taylor, E. C. 1982b. Role of microbially acquired enzymes in digestion of cellulose by desert millipedes. Applied and Environmental Microbiology. 44:281–291.

Taylor, E. C., and C. S. Crawford. 1982. Microbial gut symbionts and desert detritivores. Scientific Reviews on Arid Zone Research 1:37–52.

Tevis, L., and I. M. Newell. 1962. Studies of the biology and seasonal cycle of the giant red velvet mite, *Dinothrombium pandorae* (Acari, Trombidiidae). Ecology 43:497–505.

Tschinkel, W. R. 1972. The sorption of water vapor by windborne plant debris in the Namib Desert. Madoqua 2:63–68.

Wagner, F. H., and R. D. Graetz. 1981. Animal-animal interactions, pp. 51–83. *In:* D. W. Goodall and R. A. Perry (eds.). Arid-land ecosystems: structure, functioning and management. Vol. 2. IBP No. 17, Cambridge University Press, Cambridge, London, New York, New Rochelle, Melbourne, Sydney.

Wallwork, J. A. 1982. Desert soil fauna. Praeger, New York.

Went, F. 1969. Challenges and opportunities for desert plant physiologists, pp. 219–230. *In:* C. C. Hoff and M. J. Riedesel (eds.). Physiological systems in semiarid environments. University of New Mexico Press, Albuquerque.

Went, F. W., and M. Westergaard. 1949. Ecology of desert plants. III. Development of plants in the Death Valley National Monument, California. Ecology 30:26–38.

West, N. E. 1979. Formation, distribution and function of plant litter in desert ecosystems, pp. 647–659. *In:* D. W. Goodall and R. A. Perry (eds.). Arid-land ecosystems: Structure, functioning and management. Vol. 1. IBP No. 16, Cambridge University Press, Cambridge, London, New York, Melbourne.

Whitford, W. G. 1978. Foraging in seed-harvesting ants *Pogonomyrmex* spp. Ecology 59:185–189.

Whitford, W. G. Decomposition and nutrient cycling in deserts (this volume).

Whitford, W. G., D. W. Freckman, N. Z. Elkins, L. W. Parker, R. Parmalee, J. Phillips, and S. Tucker. 1981. Diurnal migration and responses to simulated rainfall in desert soil microarthropods and nematodes. Soil Biology and Biochemistry 13:417–425.

Wisdom, W. A., and W. G. Whitford. 1981. Effects of vegetation change on ant communities of arid rangelands. Environmental Entomology 10:893–897.

5

DECOMPOSITION AND NUTRIENT CYCLING IN DESERTS

Walter G. Whitford

New Mexico State University
Las Cruces, New Mexico

INTRODUCTION

Ecologists have generally focused on two important processes in studies of ecosystems: energy flow and nutrient cycling. Energy flow studies have demonstrated, for example, that in terrestrial ecosystems only a small percentage (10–20%) of the net aboveground primary production is consumed by herbivores as live material. The remainder, plus egesta, carcasses, and so forth, of higher trophic levels is processed by the "decomposers." The "decomposer" organisms are thus a critical part of the energy flow process; yet there is little known about "decomposers" in arid and semiarid ecosystems. Included in the "decomposers" are not only microorganisms but the whole detritivore complex (beetles, ants, millipedes, and others) and soil mesofauna for which fungi, bacteria, and yeasts serve as a source of energy.

Energy flow studies have allowed elucidation of trophic relationships, but possibly because energy is essentially an infinite resource such studies have not provided the information necessary to examine questions of system stability and to predict consequences of perturbations. Mineral nutrients are finite and all living things require a supply of these materials. There is no source of these materials outside the biosphere. Nutrients must be made available from atmospheric, soil, water, or living material stores. If the processes of death, decomposition, mineralization, and uptake occur at rates that are relatively equal, then "bottlenecks" will not occur in the system and the system will be stable. However, the processes of desertification "destabilize" arid and semiarid ecosystems. In fact, desertification may occur because rates of decomposition or mineralization are forced to diverge, resulting in "bottlenecks" and consequent

instability of the system. Reversal of "desertification" may require recon-
struction of the belowground ecosystem and reequalization of these rates.

As pointed out above, in deserts as in other ecosystems the consumption and eventual conversion to carbon dioxide, water, and minerals of the
major fraction of primary production, both above and below the ground,
occurs after the death of the plant or plant part. Thus, simply on the basis
of quantity, the processes of decomposition and mineralization of essential
elements from dead plant material represent vital processes in desert
ecosystems. In human terms, the key industry in desert ecosystems is the
production of aboveground plant biomass that can be utilized directly as a
source of food, fiber, medicine, or fuel, or utilized indirectly by domesti-
cated animals. The results of the recent International Biological Program
and other studies (Ludwig and Flavill 1979, Floret et al. 1982, Penning de
Vries and Djiteye 1982) suggest that nutrients, especially nitrogen, may
limit productivity in desert ecosystems when moisture is available. Few
studies examined decomposition processes in desert ecosystems prior to
the initiation of our work (Comanor and Staffeldt 1978), but there were
fairly extensive efforts focused on nitrogen processes in desert ecosystems
as part of the International Biological Program (West and Skujins 1978). In
this review, I will address the problem of both decomposition and nutrient cycling processes in desert ecosystems and attempt, wherever
possible, to demonstrate the relationships between these processes and
primary productivity. Since these processes are mediated via the soil
biota, I will emphasize soil biotic interactions and their importance,
where these are known or suspected.

INPUTS

In North American deserts, the evergreen shrub, *Larrea tridentata*, is
the dominant plant. There are limited data on litter fall from this species
(Burke and Dick-Peddie 1974, Strojan et al. 1979, and unpublished data).
Although there is a continuous input of senescent leaves, there are peak
periods of leaf fall that follow peak periods of vegetative productivity. In
the Chihuahuan Desert this period is in October and November, but in
the winter rainfall Mojave Desert this peak occurs in March and April
(Strojan et al. 1979). The quantity of leaf litter infall should reflect the
vegetative production of the previous growth pulse and hence be predictable based on rainfall data, but this remains to be tested and requires a
long-term data set.

Although the dominant plant in North American hot deserts is *Larrea
tridentata*, which contributes therefore the greatest mass of dead plant

material, there are other shrubs, grasses, and ephemeral plants that contribute materials to the organic matter pool. Many of the perennial shrubs are winter deciduous; hence, the abscissed leaf material is shed in one pulse at the end of the growing season. Quantities of leaf material shed should be virtually equivalent to the leaf production of the preceeding growing season. Examples of winter deciduous shrubs are mesquite (*Prosopis glandulosa*), tarbush (*Flourensia cernua*), and desert willow (*Chilopsis linearis*). In drought deciduous species, such as ocotillo (*Forqueria splendens*) and palo verde (*Cercidium* spp.), the leaf fall should provide a good measure of the leaf production of the previous growing period. In a study of litter production by the perennial shrub *Zygophyullum dumosum* in the central Negev highlands of Israel, Whitford and Steinberger (unpublished data) found that following a wet winter and spring (92.2 mm) total litter fall was 310 g ± 92 g·shrub, and following a relatively dry winter and spring (30.9 mm) total litter fall was 200 g. The primary differences between those years was that following the "wet" growing season peak litter fall of 135 g·plant^{-1} occurred in late July and August, and in the "dry" growing season peak litter fall of 85 g·plant^{-1} occurred in April. Thus, there does seem to be a relationship between quantities of perennial litter input and climatic parameters.

Perennial grasses add litter to the system but do so continually over the year. Leaves and stems die and remain as standing dead until shattered by wind or animal activity. The addition of grass fragments to the detritus pool varies seasonally. The highest rate of input is in the winter and spring months, which are the driest and windiest in the Chihuahuan Desert. In other deserts, the season of peak input of grass fragments would probably also be in the dry, windy season.

In some years the biomass production by ephemeral plants can be equal to that of woody perennials. Ephemeral plant production varies with timing and quantity of rainfall (Tevis 1958, Beatley 1969, Ludwig and Whitford 1981). The entire biomass above and below the ground enters the detritus pool in a large pulse following seed set and death of the annual plants. The quantities of organic matter added to the detritus pool from ephemerals can be a small fraction of the total or possibly more than half of the total depending upon the climatic conditions of the preceding growing season (Ludwig and Whitford 1981).

Consumers contribute to the organic matter pools in several ways. Plant sucking herbivores add a readily metabolized and carbon rich material to litter accumulations under plants in the form of honeydew excretions and excretory frass. The effect of varying levels of input of this material on decomposition rates has not been evaluated in deserts, and there are scant data from other ecosystems (Schowalter 1981, Schowalter et al. 1981). Foliage-feeding arthropods drop wastage (unconsumed portions of leaves, and so forth) and frass. This material may also contribute a significant variable to the decomposition process. However, this also remains to be measured.

We have estimated the contribution of one consumer, jackrabbits (*Lepus californicus*), to the dead plant material pool (Steinberger and Whitford 1983a). These animals prune stems from selected shrubs, eating only the fine twigs and dropping the leaves and heavier wood to the ground. The rabbits select shrubs that have a higher stem water content than the neighboring shrubs. They utilize *Ephedra* sp., *Flourensia cernua*, and *Gutierrezia sarothrae*, in addition to *L. tridentata*. The quantity of material added to the system as wastage by rabbits contributes as much as 20% of the shrub litter input. The chemistry of such leaves differs from naturally senescent leaves, as discussed in a subsequent section.

Finally, one must consider the egesta of herbivores as materials requiring decomposition and mineralization. The fecal pellets of lagomorphs (jackrabbits and cottontails) are a ubiquitous feature of soil surfaces in North American deserts. The assimilation efficiency of lagomorphs is low and varies with food quality. On a low-quality, predominately woody plant diet, jackrabbits may have an assimilation efficiency as low as 30%, therefore egesting 70% in the form of homogenized fibres mixed with gut microflora, and so forth. This material may contribute an important fraction to the detritus pool. Whitford et al. (1982) provide some data on the composition and quantities of materials in the detritus pool from a bajada with a uniform stand of creosotebush. The data are reported for samples collected in November of a year in which annual plant production was very small. Total mass under shrub canopies was 47.9 ± 38.5 g·m^{-2}: 57% *L. tridentata* leaves, 31.3% *L. tridentata* stems, and 10% rabbit feces. Total mass in open areas was 19.5 ± 26.3 g·m^{-2}: 19% *L. tridentata* leaves, 57.9% *L. tridentata* stems and 13.8% rabbit feces. Additional data of this type are needed to examine seasonal and yearly variation.

The data on standing stock of detritus exhibits the variability and spatial heterogeneity of this material in desert ecosystems. Detritus is patchy with accumulations under some shrubs, while others have virtually no litter under the canopy. Litter is redistributed by wind. Shrub clumps cause eddy currents and reduction in wind velocity that allows transported fragments to settle out, producing accumulations on the lee side of large shrubs or shrub clumps. Lighter materials like leaves are blown from intershrub spaces and accumulate in these "dead air" locations, leaving behind the heavier stem materials, fecal pellets, and so forth.

Animals also contribute to redistribution patterns. Rodents make excavations around the base of shrubs in search of food or in locating their own seed caches. These pits fill with dead plant material and subsequently are buried by wind or water. Steinberger and Whitford (1983b) estimated that 60 kg of plant material per hectare was buried in such excavations. While this represents only a small fraction of the total litter input, buried material is processed differently than material on the surface and decomposes at different rates.

Intense rains also redistribute dead plant materials on desert watersheds. Detritus is carried into rills, small streams, and larger streams by runoff. Obstructions in channels cause detritus to accumulate due to velocity reduction. These accumulations are mixed with and often covered by eroded soil, providing sites rich in organic material that become foci for soil arthropods.

Few of these processes have been quantified, and there are no models that address questions of litter inputs and rates of translocation and burial as a function of climate, yet these are important processes in desert ecosystems. As will be discussed in subsequent sections of this paper, organic matter accumulations are the source of nutrients and/or source of energy and habitat of nitrogen fixers, nitrifiers, and so forth. These patches provide the material for plant growth. A basic understanding of these processes will be necessary before we can adequately assess the stability of desert ecosystems and/or vectors of change in these systems.

CLIMATE AND DECOMPOSITION

Conventional wisdom holds that processes in deserts should vary with rainfall since deserts by definition are water-limited systems (Noy-Meir 1973, Went 1949, 1959, Beatley 1974). It was therefore surprising to find a lack of correlation between disappearance (decomposition) of leaf litter and precipitation. This lack of correlation was even more surprising in view of the fact that Meentemeyer (1978) developed a model relating decomposition to actual evapotranspiration and lignin content, and showed that this model fit the available decomposition data at the time of the publication of his papers. The data Meentemeyer used were from mesic forest ecosystems.

The first indication that decomposition in a desert ecosystem may not be coupled to precipitation and/or soil moisture came from the studies of Santos and Whitford (1981). They used combinations of insecticides and fungicides to inhibit the activity of a selected group of soil organisms, and measured mass loss of buried creosotebush leaf litter (Figure 5.1). They found that in the absence of soil fauna decomposition varied as a function of precipitation, but with soil fauna present the precipitation was a poor

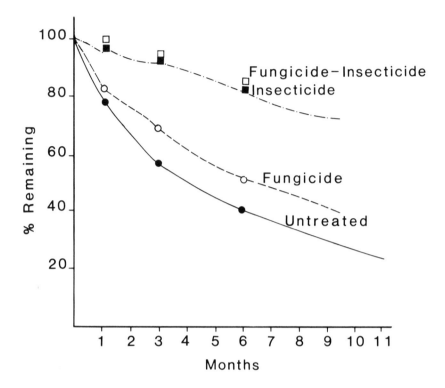

Figure 5.1 Effects of fungicides and an insecticide
(chlordane) in mass loss of buried litter in a creosote-
bush-dominated desert area. Data from Santos and
Whitford (1981).

predictor of decomposition. Plant litter on the soil surface in the Chihuahuan Desert also disappeared faster than predicted by the Meentemeyer
equation: $Y_1 = -1.31369 + 0.05350\,X_1 + 0.18472\,X_2$, where $Y_1 =$ annual
weight loss (%), $X_1 =$ annual AET (millimeters), and $X_2 =$ AET (millimeters)/Lignin (%) (Meentemeyer 1978). That equation predicted mass
loss of creosotebush leaf litter of 6.7% to 20.8% when actual mass losses
were between 40% and 90% (Whitford et al. 1981, Elkins et al. 1982, and
Whitford et al. 1982).

   Direct evidence that the rate of decomposition does not vary as a
function of rainfall in the Chihuahuan Desert has been obtained in studies
utilizing simulated rainfall. We had hypothesized that single large-quantity rain events would stimulate higher rates of decomposition than would

a series of small-quantity events that when summed equaled the single large-quantity event. We further had hypothesized that litter decomposition would be lowest on plots receiving no supplemental rainfall. The experiment was conducted for eighteen months, with one set of plots receiving 6.35 mm (0.25 inch) of supplemental water per week and other plots receiving 25.4 mm (1.0 inch) every fourth week. There were no significant differences in decomposition rates of litter attributable to the supplemental water in litter placed in the field in June. In litter placed in the field in December, the initial rates (first ninety days) were higher with water supplementation, but following that all rates were equal. That initial difference in the December litter may have been due to leaching of materials that may photooxidize in summer. Rates of decomposition were equal for the June and December litter inputs in this study (Figure 5.2).

In a comparison of mass loss of buried and surface litter in the North American hot deserts, Santos et al. (1984) found that mass loss of surface litter was better correlated with long-term average precipitation at the various study sites than with the actual precipitation during the period of study. In addition, these authors found that the disappearance of buried creosotebush leaf litter was the same in all of the hot desert areas studied, that is, approximately 40% mass loss between March and October.

Why should decomposition processes not vary as a function of actual precipitation? Litter disappearance can occur either by decomposition (solubilization of organic materials and subsequent respiration by microflora) or by ingestion and fragmentation by soil fauna. We know that the surface activity of Chihuahuan Desert subterranean termites is a seasonal phenomenon, largely restricted to August through October and depending upon the date of initiation of the "summer" rains (Whitford et al. 1983). We know also that Chihuahuan Desert subterranean termites feed in surface accumulations of creosotebush leaf litter (Whitford et al. 1983). Termite feeding could account for the large losses from surface litter and may account for much of the marked increase in rate of mass loss from creosotebush litter, such as described by Elkins et al. (1982).

While it has yet to be demonstrated that soil microfauna account for a significant fraction of the mass loss from surface litter, we do know that surface-litter accumulations provide habitat for a diverse group of microarthropods in both the Chihuahuan and Mojave deserts in North America (Wallwork 1972, Franco et al. 1979, Santos et al. 1978, Whitford et al. 1981). In surface litter the cryptostigmatid mites are numerous and may account for up to 50% of the microarthropod biomass. Cryptostigmatid (oribatid) mites have been shown to be important organisms in the breakdown of litter in forest ecosystems (Crossley 1977, Witkamp and

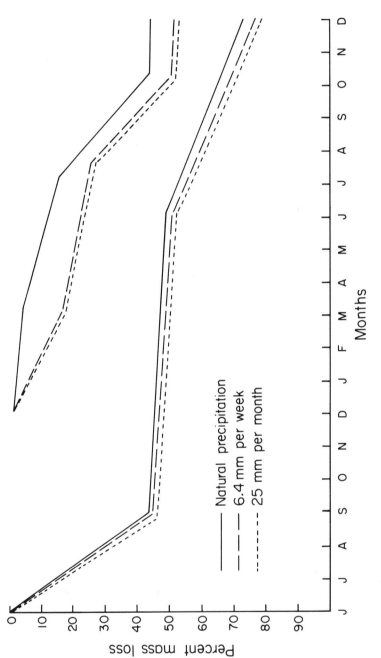

Figure 5.2 Rates of mass loss of surface litter on plots receiving supplemental rainfall (sprinkler irrigation) of 25.4 mm·month^{-1} (1 inch) in a single event or four evenly spaced events of 6.25 mm each. Based on unpublished data of Whitford, Wallwork, Freckman, and Steinberger.

Crossley 1966) by comminution (fragmentation) of litter, inoculating litter with microfloral spores and grazing on fungi. Whitford et al. (1981) found a diurnal pattern of activity of these arthropods in surface litter. For several hours in the early morning, even during the hottest and driest part of summer, oribatid mites and others were active in the litter. Thus, even in the absence of wet soil, some mite activity occurs. However, it was found that, even in wet soil, mite activity was high in the early morning and declined to nearly zero at mid-day (Whitford et al. 1981). Therefore, effectiveness in litter breakdown should vary with population numbers. Peak populations of soil microarthropods in the Chihuahuan Desert occur in August, September, and October, during and after the "normal" rainy season. This was also the period of peak litter mass loss (Whitford et al., unpublished data) in the artificial rainfall experiment.

Although the data on reproductive status of soil microarthropods from these studies are still being collected (Wallwork, personal communication), some patterns of population structure are available. Based on the occurrence of immature forms in the samples of microarthropods from under mesquite, Steinberger and Whitford (1984) concluded that, for most taxa represented, production of eggs and nymphs occurred during the "normal or predictable" wet period (from July to September in the Chihuahuan Desert). It is reasonable to assume that eggs and immatures are less resistant to dry conditions than are the heavily sclerotized adult forms. Therefore, adaptation of soil microarthropods to life in desert regions would probably involve the evolution of reproductive patterns linked to the "predictable" periods of rainfall. Such a pattern would provide the highest probability that the drought-susceptible stages will encounter soil conditions suitable for their survival. The numerical responses of soil microarthropod populations suggests that this is indeed the case. Such selective forces also explain why decomposition in other North American hot deserts varied as a function of "long-term average precipitation."

Large rainfall events outside the "normal" wet period do not seem to elicit reproductive responses in the microarthropods; hence, they have no effect on the litter breakdown processes mediated by these organisms. This lack of response to large-quantity rainfall was documented in our studies where we used artificial rainfall (Whitford et al. and Weems et al., unpublished data).

The turnover of buried litter also appears to be independent of soil moisture. Santos et al. (1984) found that buried litter in the North American hot deserts experienced approximately 40% mass loss and that there were no significant differences in mass losses in the different deserts. Although mass losses were equal, rainfall over the period of the study ranged from 8 mm to 150 mm. Santos and Whitford (1981) reported that precipitation was the most important of the seven abiotic parameters included in their multiple regression analysis of buried litter mass loss, but that explained only 40% of the variation in mass loss of untreated litter. When microarthropods were eliminated, however, mass loss was highly correlated with precipitation. Buried litter differs from surface litter in that fluctuations in abiotic parameters are attenuated. The litter quickly becomes moist and remains so even in dry soil (unpublished data) and supports populations of soil microarthropods that vary as a function of degree or state of decomposition rather than with season (Santos and Whitford 1981). Although Santos et al. (1983) reported differences in microarthropod fauna extracted from buried litter bags, there was an indication that the functional relationships between taxa were similiar. The moderate environment found belowground allows the biological processes to proceed at a rate more determined by the chemical and physical nature of the substrate than by the abiotic features of the environment.

MICROFAUNA-MICROFLORA RELATIONSHIPS

Ecosystem processes are the sum of all of the interactive processes that contribute to the larger process. For example, an apparently simple process like litter decomposition involves many subprocesses such as growth of bacteria, yeast, and fungi; grazing by protozoans and nematodes, predation, comminution of litter, translocation of litter into the soil by organisms, and so forth. When we consider the mechanics of litter breakdown and mineralization, we must then consider all of the trophic relationships of the soil biota that directly and indirectly affect the process. The soil subsystem trophic relationships are every bit as complex as those in the aboveground subsystem, involving as many as three levels of predator–prey interactions and a complex of food-web relationships that can be surmised from the kinds of organisms present.

The desert soil subsystem offers a distinct advantage to the ecologist wishing to examine decomposition–nutrient cycling processes. The system is relatively simple yet contains representatives of all major groups, thus retaining the trophic links without the complexity of a large number of taxa that seem to be doing the same thing.

The first question that needed to be answered in an examination of decomposition processes in arid ecosystems was, "What groups of soil biota are important in the decomposition process?" The answer to that question was sought by using biocides similar to those chosen by Macauley (1975) in a study of *Eucalyptus* decomposition. In our studies, when arthropods were excluded by treating buried litter with the insecticide chlordane, there was a significant (83%) reduction in mass loss (Figure 5.1). Treating litter with a combination of fungicides did not result in a significant reduction in decomposition. Fungicide-treated litter had a visible reduction in fungal hyphae, but some hyphae were present and three genera of soil fungi were isolated from the treated material (*Rhizopus*, *Alternaria* and *Cunninghamella* spp.) (Santos and Whitford 1981). A similar reduction in decomposition of buried litter treated with the insecticide chlordane was found in the other North American hot deserts (Santos et al. 1984). Thus, with respect to buried litter, microarthropods are as important in the decomposition process as they have been shown to be in more mesic systems (Edwards et al. 1970), and fungi do not appear to be as important in decomposition as has been found in more mesic systems (Macauley 1975).

By using an overlapping sequence of placing litter bags in the field and retrieving them for analysis, Santos and Whitford (1981) were able to separate seasonal effects from changes in soil fauna resulting from the changes in physical and chemical characteristics of the litter. The initial colonizers of buried litter were tydeid (or paratydeid) mites, regardless of the season of the year in which the litter was buried. Tarsonemoid mites were the next group to populate the decomposing litter. These mites are fungivores and apparently enter the litter as the fungal biomass increases. The last groups to enter the litter are the predatory gamasine mites and the generalist collembolans and psocopterans. This sequence, however, is typical only of the Chihuahuan Desert. In the comparison of buried litter decomposition in the other North American hot deserts, we found that tydeids were present in all stages of buried litter, as in the Chihuahuan Desert, but we did not find tarsonemid or pyemotid mites in any of the other deserts (Santos et al. 1983). The second stage of colonization in the other deserts was by groups of mesostigmatids. Elkins and Whitford (1982) found a similar pattern in a desert–grassland transition zone in southeastern New Mexico. Most of the microarthropod taxa extracted from buried litter are probably undescribed species, according to the taxonomic specialists to whom we have sent specimens. Therefore, the feeding habits of these taxa can only be guessed at, based on the feeding habits of related taxa that have been studied.

The trophic interactions occurring in the early stages of buried litter decomposition were studied by Santos et al. (1981b). When the tydeid mites were suppressed, the populations of bacteriophagous nematodes increased dramatically, resulting in a marked reduction in the bacteria and yeast (called bacteria by Santos et al.) populations. They found that in laboratory cultures tydeid mites were active predators on nematodes.

Thus, the regulation of decomposition in the early stages appears to be a function of predator–prey relationships. Elkins and Whitford (1982) and Santos et al. (1983) found a similar relationship between microarthropods and nematodes in other North American semiarid and arid ecosystems. Most authors have considered that regulation of decomposition and nutrient-cycling processes in ecosystems by microarthropods is mediated chiefly by oribatid mites that actually feed on dead plant material and affect decomposition by fragmentation of litter, inoculation with microbial spores, and stimulation of microflora by grazing (Crossley 1977, Edwards et al. 1970, Behan and Hill 1978). In desert ecosystems, we see rates of decomposition affected by microarthropods acting as top-level consumers (predators) as well as directly as grazers on fungi and bacteria. None of the microarthropods extracted from buried litter up to the point where 50% of the original mass is lost are related to forms that feed directly on litter or have mouth parts suitable for use of such a substrate. The tydeids could feed on yeasts, but this seems unlikely, and there is the direct evidence that they feed on nematodes. The gamasine mites are capable of preying on nematodes (Elkins and Whitford 1983) or mites, and nematodes are certainly more abundant and probably more easily captured than are the microarthropods.

Longer-term studies of decomposition of ephemeral plant litter and roots, using the same biocides, provided a similar picture of trophic relationships: early stages of decomposition occurring through the activity of bacteria and yeasts, which were grazed by protozoans and nematodes that were preyed upon by tydeid mites. Fungi become more abundant on the dead material, and tarsonemid mites and fungiphagous nematodes enter the system along with the predatory gamasine mites. Psocopterans and collembolans may enter the system and feed either directly on the plant material or on the fungi. These trophic relationships are summarized in Figure 5.3.

The studies summarized above suggest two important generalizations: (1) regulation of the rate of buried litter-root decomposition by microarthropods is indirect as suggested by Chew (1974); (2) all groups of soil organisms are important even if their role appears to be indirect.

The only studies of soil biota in surface litter in deserts have been those associated with water as a climatic variable (Santos et al. 1983, Parker et al. 1983). Assessing the development of litter arthropod communities in a desert environment is difficult because of diel variation (Whitford et al. 1981) as well as the possibility of seasonal shifts in diel activity patterns. Based on general collections made in a variety of desert environments, it is clear that litter accumulations host a variety of oribatid mites that do not seem to colonize buried litter. Genera of oribatids that are common in

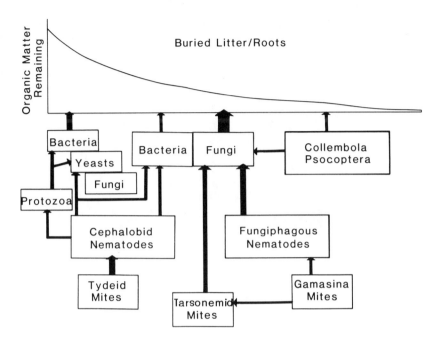

Figure 5.3 Proposed trophic relationships of soil fauna
in buried litter. The width of the arrow represents relative
quantity of organic matter or biomass consumed by the
taxa indicated in the boxes.

North American leaf litter include *Passalozetes, Galumna, Joshuella,* and
Hemilius. In addition to the oribatids, we find a variety of prostigmatid
mites, the most numerous of which are also found in buried litter, that is,
tydeids, paratydeids, tarsonemids, pyemotids, bdellids, and nanorches-
tids. When leaf litter is wet and soil is wet, collembolans may be abundant.
The collembolans are probably present all of the time but in an anhydrobiotic or cryptobiotic state; hence, they are not extracted from the litter unless
activated by water. I propose the scheme shown in Figure 5.5 for the
trophic relationships of soil microarthropods in surface-leaf accumulations.
The most important difference between functional relationships in surface
and buried litter is the contribution of oribatids to comminution of litter.
Termites also feed in surface-litter accumulations, but their activity is
seasonal and dependent upon the species composition of the litter (Whitford et al. 1982). When the soil-litter interface is moist, subterranean
termites may move significant quantities of material, as described by

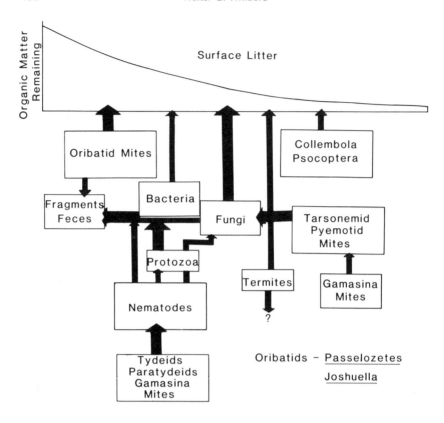

Figure 5.4 Proposed trophic relationships of soil fauna in surface litter. The width of the arrow represents relative quantity of organic matter or biomass consumed by the taxa indicated in the boxes.

Whitford et al. (1982). In the scheme proposed in Figure 5.4, the fragmented litter and feces of the microarthropods provide the substrate for the bacteria, fungi, and yeasts. Mineralization of carbon is via respiration of the soil biota. The rate of mineralization of other materials is affected by the trophic relationships in the soil. Minerals immobilized in fungal, bacterial, and yeast biomass can be released to the soil only after cell death or when cells are grazed off by higher trophic groups. In these organisms, excess nutrients are lost as excretory products. These hypothesized relationships require documentation by laboratory microcosms and by suitable field experiments.

TERMITES

Subterranean termites are diverse and abundant in the warm arid and semiarid regions of the world (Wood and Sands 1978). Wood and Sands point out that in many semiarid ecosystems the biomass and energy flow through termites is greater than or equal to that of mammals, including grazing herbivores. In desert grassland areas of southern New Mexico, I estimated that subterranean termite biomass exceeded the biomass of domestic livestock at current stocking rates by a factor of 10. This was a conservative estimate because it was based on numbers of termites feeding in surface baits (Johnson and Whitford 1975). Based solely on abundance, it is obvious that termites are important components of desert ecosystems, and when the contributions of termites to the overall "economy" of such systems is examined, termites can be viewed as "keystone" taxa. Paine (1969 a and b) first applied the term *keystone* to species that affected changes in community trophic structure. A "keystone" taxon in an ecosystem is one that maintains system stability by affecting both biotic and abiotic processes. In the Chihuahuan Desert we have considerable data that indicate the "keystone" importance of subterranean termites.

In the absence of termites, physical weathering and activity of fungi and bacteria accounted for only 4% mass loss from dung pats during the growing season. Dung pats attacked by termites completely disintegrated and mixed with soil in the next heavy rainfall or by wind action following colonization by termite foragers. If termites were eliminated from such an ecosystem, dung would require from twenty-five to thirty years to be reincorporated into the soil. The accumulation of organic matter into dung and the physical presence of increasing quantities of this material would markedly reduce the productivity of semiarid rangelands for grazing livestock.

Termites not only consume dung but a variety of other plant materials, especially ephemeral plants and grasses. Some ephemeral plants apparently are less palatable to termites than others, possibly due to material toughness (Whitford et al. 1982). During the short period when subterranean termites forage on the surface in the Chihuahuan Desert, they remove significant quantities of preferred plant materials (Figure 5.5). In years when grasses and forbs are not extremely abundant, subterranean termites consume creosotebush *L. tridentata* leaves at rates similar to grasses and forbs, but in years when alternate foods are abundant the termites apparently do not utilize the creosotebush leaf litter (Fowler and Whitford 1980). Subterranean termites are also essential for the breakdown of certain woody materials in this ecosystem (Whitford et al. 1982).

Based on data from the Sahel in Africa and some data from Australia, Wood and Sands (1978) provide evidence that termites are "keystone"

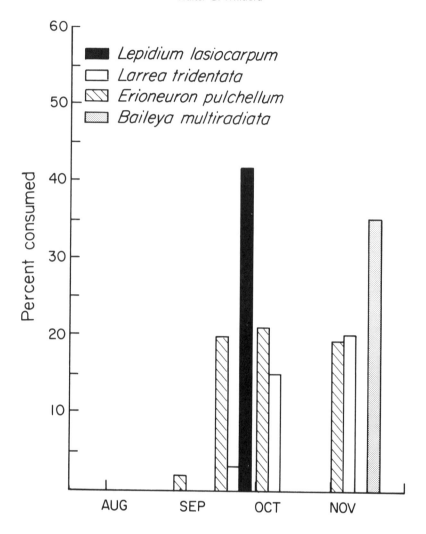

Figure 5.5 Percentage of selected plant materials removed from surface accumulations by subterrarrean termites. The percentage removed by termites was obtained by subtracting mass loss on plots where termites
were removed from mass loss on plots where termites
were present. Details in Whitford et al. 1982.

taxa in other arid and semiarid ecosystems. Termites are not only abundant but change the physical and chemical characteristics of the soil process, consume a major fraction of the primary productivity, and return nutrients to the ecosystem via salivary secretions, feces, corpses, and predators. Based on studies of lizard communities, it is evident that termites are "keystone" taxa with respect to higher tropic levels (Pianka 1973). In the Kalahari, Australian, and North American deserts, termites make up a significant fraction of the diets of lizards.

The importance of termites in semiarid and arid ecosystems is not limited to organic matter processing and nutrient cycling. Nest construction, galleries, and tunnels all affect soil structure and soil chemistry. The walls of nests and gallery tunnels are soil particles cemented with saliva. Aboveground nests and carton built around food items are made of soil particles from a lower horizon that have been transported to the surface. The large quantities of material turned over by this kind of activity can be very significant (Wood and Sands 1978). In experiments where termites were eliminated from a desert area (Elkins et al. 1984), infiltration rates were reduced and particle-size distribution of sediment in the runoff was different from plots where termites were present (Figure 5.6). These changes in hydrological characteristics of soils attributable to termites have an effect on the vegetation. Parker et al. (1982) and Whitford et al. (1982) document differences in vegetation attributable to termite removal. There was a quantitative reduction in biomass of fluff-grass and qualitative differences in ephemeral plants on plots where termites were removed.

The studies utilizing plots where termites were eliminated provide convincing evidence as to the "keystone" position of termites in the structure of a desert ecosystem. Empirical studies of other animal taxa may show that these are as important as "regulators" of processes and effectors of structural integrity as are termites. The studies documenting these relationships in the Chihuahuan Desert were initiated in 1977 and are continuing at present. The value of long-term experiments in arid ecosystems and others is only now beginning to be appreciated. We will undoubtedly learn a great deal about what it is that provides ecosystem stability, how disturbed ecosystems recover, and what characteristics make some organisms "keystones" in ecosystems as more ecologists make the commitment to long-term manipulative studies.

NUTRIENT CYCLING

It has recently been documented that desert soils are characterized by low concentrations of nitrogen, phosphorus, and organic matter (West

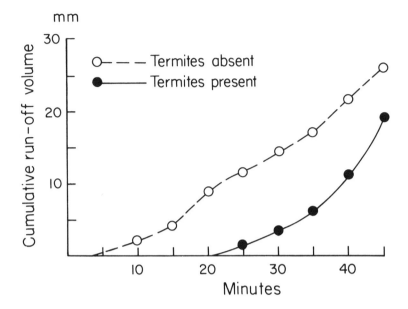

Figure 5.6 A comparison of runoff on plots with termites present and plots where termites have been removed. Runoff values obtained using rainfall simulator
and 1 m² plots having from 7 to 10% vegetative cover.
Plots were adjacent plots on the same sandy soil on a
desert bajada at the New Mexico State University
Ranch. Based on data in Elkins 1983.

1981). A growing number of studies point to nutrient limitation as a factor
limiting plant production (Cline and Rickard 1973, Floret et al. 1982,
Penning de Vries and Djiteye 1982).

It has been suggested that the low nutrient capacity of desert soils
results in part from the origin of parent materials, that is, weathering of
primary minerals forming kaolinitic clays. Kaolinitic clays retain minerals
less than other clay types, and this, combined with low humic acid
content, makes mineral exchange poor (West 1981). Our data on decomposition and turnover of roots (Parker et al. 1983, Stinnett and Whitford
unpublished data) show that these rates are so high that humic materials,
if formed, are quickly metabolized by the soil organisms that are energy-
limited. Even when organic materials are mineralized, thus providing
nutrients for plant growth, the low nitrification potentials of desert sandy

soils and the low exchange rates result in volatilization of nitrogen (Skujins 1981). Leaching is rarely sufficient to remove the more abundant ions resulting in salinization, alkalization, and calcification of the soils. Evaporation pulls many elements from deeper in the soil profile toward the surface, resulting in accumulations of calcium carbonate and calcium sulfate forming petrocalcic or gypsic layers (caliche). These layers may inhibit water percolation and root growth into deeper soil layers.

These factors combine to produce a pattern of mineral distribution in which mineral nutrients are concentrated in the upper 5 cm of soil and under shrub canopies or areas of organic matter accumulation. Soils deeper than 5 cm tend to be nutrient poor (Nishita and Haug 1973, West and Klemmedson 1978, Skujins 1981). The distribution of nitrogen in arid soils is closely tied to organic matter; hence, it is greatest in areas of aboveground and belowground carbon accumulation (Skujins 1981).

In North American deserts, it has been well established that annual plants are concentrated under shrub canopies (Muller 1953, Patten 1978, Parker et al. 1982). Litter accumulates under shrub canopies, producing a soil with higher organic matter, higher nutrient levels, and enhanced water infiltration. These factors combine to support luxuriant growth of annual plants under the canopy. The low nutrient levels in the intershrub spaces, lower infiltration, and harsher thermal environment combine to produce sparse annual plants in these areas. Shrubs with litter layers are the "islands of fertility" in a shrub-dominated desert. However, the paucity of essential nutrients, plus the favourable water status and thermal environment, combine to produce what may be rate-limiting conditions on plant growth, even with adequate or above "normal" water inputs.

In studies of *Larrea tridentata* growth using irrigation we found that irrigated shrubs added little more biomass than nonirrigated shrubs. Cunningham and Reynolds (personal communication) attribute this to a nitrogen limitation. Parker et al. (1983) found that considerable nitrogen was accumulated and immobilized by fungi on dead roots of the desert annual *Lepidium lasiocarpum*. They hypothesized that the rapid growth and death of annual plants in one wet period would result in N immobilization via fungi on decomposing annual plant roots, thereby reducing available N to the shrub and/or annual plants during the next wet period. Annual plant roots extend into the rooting zone of *Larrea* shrubs (unpublished data). Fungi growing on these roots are probably better able to scavange available N than are the roots of the shrub which undoubtedly require lower soil water potentials to obtain available N. The mineralization of that fungus immobilized N involves grazing by nematodes and microarthropods, and is probably water pulsed; hence, it is more sporadic than is the mass loss from the dead plant material. Our long-term rainfall simulation studies provide data on vegetative growth consistent with this hypothesis. We have found, for example, that shrubs receiving 330 mm supplemental rainfall per year have significantly lower leaf and stem and bud nitrogen than do shrubs receiving no supplemental water. The results of these studies are consistent with the view that most of the N for plant production in a desert is from internal cycling and not by fixation by free living N fixing soil flora, root symbionts, by cyanobacteria, or by atmospheric deposition. However, these potential inputs need to be studied and will be examined briefly in this review.

If an ecosystem is stable, nutrient losses must be balanced by nutrient inputs. If inputs exceed losses, the system is aggrading with respect to that particular nutrient. Nitrogen is recognized as the most probably limiting nutrient in deserts when there is adequate water for plant growth. The pathways by which nitrogen can enter and leave the system are complex, and not all pathways have received equal attention.

Nitrogen may enter a system through atmospheric dust (translocation) or by N fixed by the energy of electrical storms from atmospheric N_2 (Loftis and Kurtz 1980). West (1978) estimated that from 4 to 6 kg·ha^{-1}·yr^{-1} nitrogen was input via precipitation (the sum of the abovementioned processes) in the Great Basin Desert. West calculated that these physical inputs could account for from 20 to 50% of the new N entering the ecosystem. These figures may be conservative when we consider the hot deserts where most of the precipitation is from convectional storms and where electrostatic discharges could fix considerably more N. We have found, for example, that standing dead wood supports fungi that accumulate N producing a layer of N rich wood on the surface of stems that is then consumed by termites (MacKay and Whitford unpublished data). There must be an atmospheric source of this N. Based on these observations, I feel that the estimates for the Great Basin are much lower than physical N inputs in the Chihuahuan Desert. We are in the process of collecting these data at present under the auspices of the NSF-Long Term Ecological Research Program.

Symbiotic nitrogen fixation by *Rhizobium* or free-living rhizosphere organisms needs to be measured in desert ecosystems. Noy-Meir (1974) and Hadley and Szarek (1981) point out that this process occurs in legumenous and other desert plants and could be substantial, but that assessment is based on scant data. Other types of plant-bacteria-fungi associations could fix nitrogen (see review by Farnsworth et al. 1981), but there are no substantive studies that provide the basis for evaluating the relative importance of this input.

Cryptogamic soil crusts (cyanobacteria and lichens) may make significant amounts of nitrogen available to plants (Raushforth and Brothuson 1983). Where cryptogamic crusts form they may also enhance water infiltration. Studies in the Great Basin (Rychert et al. 1978, Klubek and Skujins 1980, Snyder and Wullstein 1973) have shown that cryptogamic crusts fix nitrogen at soil moistures close to field capacity. This was confirmed by Eskew and Ting (1978) in the southern Mojave Desert. Although cryptogamic crusts may fix quantities of nitrogen, that nitrogen is used in the growth of the cryptogams and hence is not readily available for growth of vascular plants. It therefore seems likely that grazers on the crusts provide a mechanism by which N_2 fixed by algal-lichen crusts can be mineralized and made available to plants. Based on microcosm studies, Hanlon and Anderson (1979) and Coleman et al. (1977) have shown that grazers increase the mineralization of nutrients. Ghabbour et al. (1980), in laboratory studies of one month duration, found that under certain conditions grazers (protozoans and nematodes) stimulated nitrogen fixation by cyanobacteria. They concluded that "extrapolations from sterilized laboratory experiments to field conditions are not feasible." However, based on the work cited above, it does appear that grazers may play an important role in N mineralization from cryptogamic crusts. These grazers include protozoans and nematodes and also certain soil acari like nanorchestid mites. We are currently examining some of these relationships in both field and laboratory studies.

Although there is an increasing body of evidence that nitrogen may limit productivity in desert ecosystems, and we have at least some information on nitrogen cycling in these systems, there is virtually no information on other nutrients (West 1981). The element other than nitrogen most frequently mentioned as potentially limiting productivity is phosphorus. The alkaline calcic and gypsic soils characteristic of desert systems may tie up phosphorus insoluble forms so that phosphorus may not be available even in soils with adequate levels of this element. In the Australian arid zone the soils contain insufficient phosphorus (Beadle 1966). Since phosphorus is required in DNA synthesis and in ATP, all organisms including nitrogen fixers and decomposer microflora require this element. Therefore, soil factors that affect the availability of phosphorus can indirectly affect nitrogen fixation and the nitrogen cycle, plus the cycling of all other minerals. It is therefore evident that the biogeochemistry of phosphorus needs attention in arid regions.

As human development of arid and semiarid regions increases so do concentrations of minerals in atmospheric dust and as atmospheric gases. Desert regions in the air sheds of major metropolitan areas may experience enhanced inputs of sulphates and nitrates from anthropogenic sources. Rainfall may have a lowered pH. Acidic rainfall could have broad significations in arid and semiarid regions and may even be beneficial in reducing soil pH and making elements available that are unavailable at alkaline soil pH. Unfortunately, we have only the most rudimentary understanding of nutrient cycling processes in desert ecosystems and are as yet unable to make predictions concerning the influence of such changes on the structure and function of desert ecosystems. Therein lies an important challenge to desert ecologists.

REFERENCES

Beadle, N. C. W. 1966. Soil phosphate and its role in molding segments of the Australian flora and vegetation with special reference to xeromorphy and sclerophylly. Ecology 47:991–1007.

Beatley, J. C. 1969. Dependence of desert rodents on winter annuals and precipitation. Ecology 50:721–724.

Beatley, J. C. 1974. Phenological events and their environmental triggers in Mojave desert ecosystems. Ecology 55:856–863.

Behan, V. M., and S. B. Hill. 1978. Feeding habits and spore dispersal of Oribatid mites in the North American Arctic. Revue d'Ecologie et Biologie du Sol 15(4):497–516.

Burk, J. H., and W. A. Dick-Peddie. 1973. Comparative production of *Larrea divaricata* Cov. on three geomorphic surfaces in southern New Mexico. Ecology 54:1094–1102.

Chew, R. M. 1974. Consumers as regulators of ecosystems: an alternative to energetics. Ohio Journal of Science 74:359–370.

Cline, J. F., and W. H. Richard. 1973. Hebage yields in relation to soil water and assimilated nitrogen. Journal of Range Management 26:296–298.

Coleman, D. C., C. V. Cole, R. V. Anderson, M. Blaha, M. K. Campion, M. Clarholm, E. T. Elliott, H. W. Hunt, B. Shaefer, and J. Sinclair. 1977. An analysis of rhizosphere-saprophage interactions in terrestrial ecosystems. *In:* U. Lohn, and T. Persson (eds.). Proceedings of VI Colloquium of Soil Zoology. NFR Bulletin No. 25, Uppsala, Sweden.

Comanor, P. L., and E. E. Staffeldt. 1978. Decomposition of plant litter in two western North American deserts, pp. 31–49. *In:* N. E. West and J. J. Skujins (eds.). Nitrogen in Desert Ecosystems. US/IBP Synthesis Series 9. Dowden, Hutchinson, and Ross; Stroudsburgh, Pennsylvania.

Crossley, D. A., Jr. 1977. The role of terrestrial saprophagous arthropods in forest soils: current status of concepts, pp. 49–56. *In:* W. J. Mattson (ed.). The role of arthropods in forest ecosystems, Springer-Verlag, New York.

Edwards, C. A., D. E. Reichle, and D. A. Crossley, Jr. 1970. The role of soil invertebrates in turnover of organic matter and nutrients, pp. 147–172. *In:* D. E. Reichle (ed.). Ecological studies. Vol. 16, Analysis of Temperate Forest Ecosystems, Spring, New York.

Elkins, N. Z., and W. G. Whitford. 1982. The role of microarthropods and nematodes in decomposition in a semi-arid ecosystem. Oecologia 55:303–310.

Elkins, N. Z., Y. Steinberger, and W. G. Whitford. 1982. Factors affecting the applicability of the AET model for decomposition in arid environments. Ecology 63:579–580.

Elkins, N. Z., George V. Sabol, Timothy J. Ward, and W. G. Whitford. 1986. The influence of subterranean termites on the hydrological characteristics of a Chihuahuan desert ecosystem. Oecologia. In press.

Farnsworth, R. B., E. M. Romney, and A. Wallace. 1978. Nitrogen fixation by microflora—higher plant associations in arid to semi-arid environments, pp. 17–19. *In:* N. E. West and J. Skujins (eds.). Nitrogen in Desert Ecosystems. US/IBP Series 9. Dowden, Hutchinson, and Ross; Stroudsburg, Pennsylvania.

Floret, C., R. Pontanier and S. Rambal. 1982. Measurement and modelling of primary production and water use in a south Tunisian steppe. Journal of Arid Environments 5:77–90.

Fowler, H. G., and W. G. Whitford. 1980. Termites, microarthropods and the decomposition of senescent and fresh creosotebush (*Larrea tridentata*) leaf litter. Journal of Arid Environments 3:1–6.

Franco, P. J., E. B. Edney, and J. F. McBrayer. 1979. The distribution and abundance of soil arthropods in the northern Mojave desert. Journal of Arid Environments 2:137–149.

Ghabbour, S. I., E. Y. El-Ayouty, M. S. Khadr, and A-M. S. El-Ton. 1980. Grazing by microfauna and productivity of heterocystous nitrogen-fixing blue-green algae in desert soils. Oikos 34:209–218.

Hadley, N. F., and S. R. Szarek. 1981. Productivity of desert ecosystems. BioScience 31:747–753.

Hanlon, R. D. G., and J. M. Anderson. 1979. The effects of collembola grazing on microbial activity in decomposing leaf litter. Oecologia 38:93–99.

Johnson, K. A., and W. G. Whitford. 1975. Foraging ecology and relative importance of subterranean termites in Chihuahuan desert ecosystems. Environmental Entomology 4:66–70.

Klubek, B., and J. Skujins. 1980. Heterotrophic N_2-fixation in arid soil crusts. Soil Biology and Biochemistry 12:229–236.

Loftis, S. G., and E. B. Kurtz. 1980. Field studies of inorganic nitrogen added to semi-arid soils by rainfall and blue-green algae. Soil Science 129:150–155.

Ludwig, J. A., and P. Flavill. 1979. Productivity patterns of *Larrea* in the northern Chihuahuan desert, pp. 139–150. *In:* E. C. Lopez, T. J. Mabry, and S. F. Tavizon (eds.). Larrea. Centro de Investigacion en Quimica Aplicada, Saltillo, Mexico.

MacCauley, B. J. 1975. Biodegradation of litter in *Eucalyptus pauciflora* communities. I. Techniques for comparing the effects of fungi and insects. Soil Biology and Biochemistry 17:341–344.

Meentemeyer, V. 1978. Macroclimate and lignin control of litter decomposition rates. Ecology 59(3):465–472.

Nishita, H., and R. M. Haug. 1973. Distribution of different forms of nitrogen in some desert soils. Soil Science 116:51–58.

Noy-Meir, I. 1973. Desert ecosystems: environment and producers, pp. 25–52. *In:* R. F. Johnston (ed.). Annual Review of Ecology and Systematics. Annual Review, Palo Alto, California.

Noy-Meir, I. 1974. Desert ecosystems: higher trophic levels. Annual Review Ecology and Systematics 5:195–214.

Paine, R. T. 1969a. A note on trophic complexity and community stability. American Naturalist 10391–93.

Paine, R. T. 1969b. The *Pisaster-Tegula* interaction: prey patches, predator food preference and intertidal community structure. Ecology 50:950–961.

Parker, L. W., H. G. Fowler, G. Ettershank, and W. G. Whitford. 1982. The effects of subterranean termite removal on desert soil nitrogen and ephemeral flora. Journal of Arid Environments 5:53–59.

Parker, L. W., P. F. Santos, J. Phillips, and W. G. Whitford. 1984. Carbon and nitrogen dynamics during the decomposition of litter and roots of a Chihuahuan desert annual. Ecological Monographs 54:339–360.

Penning de Vries, F. W. T., and M. A. Djiteye. 1982. La productivitie des paturages saheliens. Centre for Agricultural Publishing and Documentation, Wageningen.

Pianka, E. R. 1973. The structure of lizard communities, pp. 53–74. *In:* R. F. Johnston (ed.). Annual Review of Ecology and Systematics, Annual Review, Palo Alto, California.

Rushforth, S. R., and J. D. Brotherson. 1982. Cryptogamic soil crusts in the deserts of North America. The American Biology Teacher 44:472–475.

Rychert, R., J. Skujins, D. Sorensen, and D. Porcella. 1978. Nitrogen fixation by lichens and free-living microorganisms in deserts, pp. 20–30. *In:* N. E. West, and J. Skujins (eds.). Nitrogen in Desert Ecosystems. US/IBP Synthesis Series 9, Dowden, Hutchinson, and Ross; Stroudsburg, Pennsylvania.

Santos, P. F., E. DePree, and W. G. Whitford. 1978. Spatial distribution of litter and microarthropods in a Chihuahuan desert ecosystem. Journal of Arid Environments 1:41–48.

Santos, P. F., and W. G. Whitford. 1981. The effects of microarthropods on litter decomposition in a Chihuahuan desert ecosystem. Ecology 62:654–663.

Santos, P. F., J. Phillips, and W. G. Whitford. 1981b. The role of mites and nematodes in early stages of buried litter decomposition in a desert. Ecology 62:664–669.

Santos, P. F., N. Z. Elkins, Y. Steinberger, and W. G. Whitford. 1984. A comparison of surface and buried *Larrea tridentata* leaf litter decomposition in North American hot deserts. Ecology 65:278–284.

Schowalter, T. D., J. W. Webb, and D. A. Crossley, Jr. 1981. Community structure and nutrient content of canopy arthropods in clear cut and uncut forest ecosystems. Ecology 62:1010–1019.

Schowalter, T. D. 1981. Insect herbivore relationship to the state of the host plant: Biotic regulation of ecosystem nutrient cycling through ecological succession. Oikos 37:126–130.

Skujins, J. 1981. Nitrogen cycling in arid ecosystems. Ecological Bulletin (Stockholm) 33:477–491.

Snyder, J. M., and L. H. Wullstein. 1973. The role of desert cryptograms in nitrogen fixation. American Midland Naturalist 90:257–265.

Strojan, C. L, F. B. Turner, and R. Castetter. 1979. Litter fall from shrubs in the northern Mojave desert. Ecology 60:891–900.

Steinberger, Y., and W. G. Whitford. 1984. Spatial and temporal relationships of soil microarthropods on a desert watershed. Pedobiologia 26:275–284.

Wallwork, J. A. 1972. Mites and other microarthropods from the Joshua tree national monument, California. Journal of Zoology (London) 168:91–105.

Went, F. W. 1949. Ecology of desert plants. II. The effect of rain and temperature on germination and growth. Ecology 30:1–13.

West, N. E. 1981. Nutrient cycling in desert ecosystems, pp. 301–324. *In:* D. A. Goodall, and R. A. Perry (eds.). Arid Land Ecosystems: Structure, functioning and manage ment. Vol. 2. Cambridge University Press.

West, N. E., and J. Skujins. 1978. Nitrogen in Desert Ecosystems. US/IBP Synthesis Series 9, Dowden, Hutchinson and Ross, Stroudsburg, Pennsylvania.

Whitford, W. G., Y. Steinberger, and G. Ettershank. 1982. Contributions of subterranean termites to the "economy" of Chihuahuan desert ecosystems. Oecologia 55:298–302.

Whitford, W. G., R. Repass, L. W. Parker, and N. Z. Elkins. 1982. Effects of initial litter accumulation and climate on litter disappearance in a desert ecosystem. American Midland Naturalist 108:105–110.

Whitford, W. G., D. W. Freckman, N. Z. Elkins, L. W. Parker, R. Parmalee, J. Phillips, and S. Tucker. 1981. Diurnal migration and responses to simulated rainfall in desert soil microarthropods and nematodes. Soil Biology and Biochemistry 13:417–425.

Whitford, W. G., V. Meentemeyer, T. R. Seastedt, K. Cromack, Jr., D. A. Crossley, P. Santos, R. L. Todd, and J. B. Waide. 1981a. Exceptions to the AET model: Deserts and clear-cut forests. Ecology 62:275–277.
Witkamp, M., and D. A. Crossley, Jr. 1966. The role of arthropods and microflora in breakdown of white oak litter. Pedobiologia 6:293–303.
Wood, T. G., and W. A. Sands. 1978. The role of termites in ecosystems, pp. 245–292. *In:* M. V. Brian (ed.). Production Ecology of Ants and Termites. Cambridge University Press, Cambridge, Great Britain.

6

STRUCTURE AND DYNAMICS OF DESERT STREAMS

Stuart G. Fisher

Arizona State University
Tempe, Arizona

INTRODUCTION

The label "desert stream" is something of a misnomer. Except for organisms in saline waters, the biota of streams in deserts face none of the special problems of maintaining water balance which are so formidable to their terrestrial neighbors. Desert conditions do not exist within freshwater ecosystems of terrestrial deserts, yet the arid terrestrial context shapes conditions for life in embedded aquatic systems in several significant ways. Streams in deserts are thus substantially different from their counterparts in more mesic regions.

Other types of aquatic environments also exist in deserts—playas, rock pools (*tinajas*), cattle tanks, small natural lakes, and large artificial reservoirs. None, however, is as extensive or as ancient as the desert stream. Most native fishes of the desert Southwest, for example, are spring and stream fishes, attesting to the long continuous history of running water ecosystems of this region.

Rather than present a travelogue emphasizing differences among southwestern streams, I will generalize from the typical composite desert stream, emphasizing regional similarities, which will then be compared and contrasted with streams elsewhere. My basic contention is that desert streams provide a great opportunity to further our general understanding of stream ecosystem structure and function. They do this by extending the range of conditions under which ecosystem generalities are to apply, and thereby provide both a test and a challenge to ecosystem paradigms of often distinctly mesic bias. The first step in the illustration of this point is to describe the mesic stream paradigm.

STRUCTURE AND FUNCTION OF MESIC STREAMS

Much of what we know of streams as ecosystems has come from studies of streams in northern and eastern North America. With the exception of a few outliers, stream research has been concentrated in the region from New England to Georgia in the South and Minnesota in the West, the Rockies and Sierra Nevada, and the Pacific Northwest. Smaller streams in these regions share many attributes.

Abundant precipitation generates a lotic ecosystem, which is continuous in space and time with perpetual connectedness between all stream orders during all seasons of the year. Well-wetted adjacent terrestrial systems provide vegetative cover (usually trees) to the stream bank, shading the stream and thereby greatly reducing *in situ* photosynthesis. Organic inputs are high and occur as leaf material from this riparian zone. The economy of these mesic streams is thus largely dependent upon allochthonous detritus (Fisher and Likens 1973). Aquatic macroconsumers (largely immature insects) use this material in many ways. Shredders eat leaf-size material directly, collector-gatherers consume fine particles either from sediment deposits or after removal from suspension by various filtering mechanisms. Microorganisms such as fungi and bacteria also contribute to detrital decay by softening leaf tissues, reducing particle size, increasing nitrogen content, and in so doing, "conditioning" allochthonous detritus and rendering it more palatable to macroconsumers (Petersen and Cummins 1974, Suberkropp et al. 1976). Attendant microorganisms are themselves ingested and thereby contribute to invertebrate secondary production. Recent work has shown that algal productivity provides high quality food to consumers (Anderson and Cummins 1979, Rounick et al. 1982), yet rates are low and the trophic structure of mesic streams is overwhelmingly dependent on allochthonous detritus from the adjacent terrestrial forest.

Because of this low quality detrital food (high C:N) and, in high latitude streams, low temperature, invertebrate growth rates are comparatively low and most insects are univoltine (one generation per year). As a result, the invertebrate fauna turns over slowly, with annual production to biomass ratios of from 2 to 5 (Waters 1969).

Dynamics of inorganic nutrients in mesic streams are poorly known. Study of nutrient cycling in streams is difficult because longitudinal transport strongly influences temporal cycling at a given site, and tributary inputs confound mass balance budgets. Progress in nutrient "spiraling" in streams has been recent (Webster 1975, Newbold et al. 1981), and has emphasized phosphorus, which often limits primary production in streams and lakes of mesic areas. Since primary production is low, the relevance of nutrients to mesic streams lies largely in the microbial augmentation of decomposing leaves with nutrients. Nitrogen is the element that has received most attention in this regard, yet seldom in the context of spiraling models. As we shall see, the study of nutrient dynamics is, in many ways, more tractable in streams of desert regions.

Streams everywhere flood; however, northern and eastern streams show gradually rising hydrographs. Except for low gradient or Great Plains streams, bottom materials of small mesic streams are relatively stable and are subject to movement during only the largest floods. Flooding takes its toll on stream biota, yet univoltine and semivoltine insects and longer-lived fishes are common and evidently can cope with frequent flooding of this quality and magnitude. While recovery following disturbance (for example, forest succession) is a common theme in ecosystem ecology, successional paradigms have gained little following in the realm of stream ecology.

Finally, the gradual change in stream structure and function along the headwater to large river gradient has become a strong organizing paradigm under the River Continuum aegis of Vannote et al. (1980). Upstream reaches differ from downstream reaches in several predictable ways in terms of energy flow, community structure, and other important features. Most of these are related to organic matter inputs and processing, which obviously have a strong longitudinal component in running waters. It is as yet uncertain whether observed longitudinal patterns result from upstream influences on downstream components or from morphometric changes accompanying downstream flow (decreased slope, greater depth, more open canopy, and so forth). Both of these factors are probably relevant, but are difficult to separate experimentally.

STREAMS OF THE DESERT SOUTHWEST

Given the mesic paradigm, we might ask how desert streams measure up. I would like to make a few comparisons, especially where desert streams do not fit the mesic mold. First, though, it is necessary to describe the major physical features of the typical desert stream. The desert is replete with stream channels; however, most of these transport water for only minutes to days following substantial rainfall. Only large watersheds contain water perennially. For example, Sycamore Creek, a perennial stream near Phoenix, Arizona, drains a watershed of 505 km^2. Elevations therein range from 427 to 2164 m and precipitation from 30 to 75 cm/yr, yet modal summer flow is only 0.03 m^3/s and much of the main stream channel is dry in summer. This is because potential evaporation exceeds annual precipitation by approximately tenfold, at least at lower

CROSS SECTION:

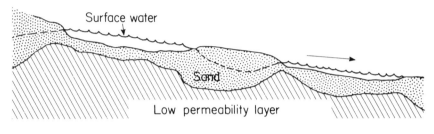

AERIAL VIEW:

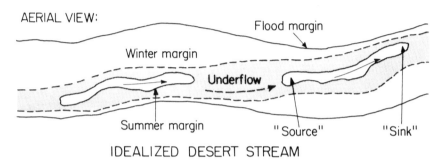

IDEALIZED DESERT STREAM

Figure 6.1 Generalized morphology of a small desert stream. In winter, surface flow is continuous but summer surface flow is evident only between source and sink defining discrete segments of fifty to several hundred meters length. Spatial pattern depends upon bedrock contours and the amount and distribution of sand in the stream channel.

elevations. The stream is hydrologically flashy, responding rapidly to summer storm events with "wall of water" flash floods up to 50 m³/s (Fisher and Minckley 1978). Flow during nonflood periods is supported by the slow release of water from storage (summer and winter rains and snow melt from higher elevations) (Thomsen and Schumann 1968). In desert regions virtually no perennial streams exist which are not fed by runoff from higher, more mesic regions in the watershed.

These features generate a stream quite different physically from its mesic counterpart. The main stream channel is wide, shaped largely by rare flooding events. Similarly, the usually sparse riparian vegetation is restricted to the periphery of the flood channel, while the broad, shallow modal-flow channel wanders over the alluvium, often some distance from the riparian vegetation. Furthermore, the unglaciated terrain provides little silt and clay to the stream, so water is exceptionally clear. Insolation to the stream bottom is thus nearly as high as to the terrestrial desert surface. Potential for *in situ* photosynthesis is therefore considerable.

The channel where perennial surface flow first appears in a typical desert drainage is one of high order (sensu Strahler 1957), perhaps 6 to 10. Stream channels of the same low orders (1–4) that characterize mesic streams are dry most of the year. Yet the site of first appearance of surface flow defines stream order. First-order desert streams (that is, headwaters) may occur in eighth-order channels, and thus are considered "underfit."

Stream bottom sediment is largely sand and fine gravel, of variable thickness (up to several meters), underlain by less permeable strata. Where sediments are deep and discharge is low, flow may occur only below the sediment surface. Flow emerges when underlying bedrock is shallow, but percolates back into the sand where bedrock recedes. This results in spatial intermittency which breaks surface water into discrete isolated segments of a few to several hundred meters between "source" and "sink" (Figure 6.1). The extent of spatial intermittency is a function of channel morphometry and discharge, and is most common in summer.

These characteristic physical features go far in explaining the major differences between mesic and desert streams. I will attempt to outline these differences in greater detail in the following considerations of desert stream energetics, nutrient dynamics, and, finally, response to disturbance by flooding. In each of these cases, results will be compared to the mesic paradigm and suggestions made for construction of more general stream paradigms.

ENERGETICS OF DESERT STREAMS

Allochthonous Inputs

Leaf litter input to headwater mesic streams may approach 1.5 kg/m^2 annually, but decreases downstream as the stream widens and the canopy opens (Fisher and Likens 1973, Fisher 1977). Mathews and Kowalczewski (1969) report litter production rates of 1588 g per linear meter of stream bank; however, areal inputs (per m^2) decrease as a function of stream width. Large rivers lined with trees receive a constant annual input of leaves per linear meter but an ever decreasing input per unit stream bottom area as they flow toward the sea. Litter input to desert streams has never been measured, but there are several reasons to think it low.

Riparian vegetation is discontinuous along many desert watercourses and often consists of a single rank of trees; thus, linear input rates are probably reduced and are not augmented by aeolian transport of leaves from upslope. Second, much litter fall impinges on the dry channel. As leaves blow into streams but seldom blow out, the desert stream may receive a higher areal leaf litter input than the adjacent dry channel; however, this remains small compared to the mesic situation. Perhaps the greatest impediment to terrestrial litter use in desert streams is not low input but limited storage. Cummins (1974) points out that retention devices such as snags are necessary to retain leaves in Michigan streams. Boulders, branches, and tree roots snag leaves which form packs or accumulations, but this structure is absent from most sandy desert streams. Large woody debris, important in generating organic dams in forest streams (Bilby and Likens 1980, Keller and Swanson 1979, Naiman and Sedell 1979), is limited in deserts and is too small to obstruct wide desert channels. Even if leaves were to enter in large amounts, they would be readily exported when discharge increased and water rose. Exported material is either washed far downstream or is entrained in the adjacent floodplain where snags abound. Whatever the case, shredding insects are extremely rare in desert streams like Sycamore Creek. Leaf packs which do occur are devoid of shredders capable of using this resource directly. Therefore, because of the physical characteristics of the desert stream ecosystem, leaf litter is not present long enough for leaf shredders to complete their life cycles, and none exist.

This is not to say that allochthonous organic matter is unimportant in deserts. Leaf material may serve as temporary habitat for macroinvertebrates, such as snails and blackflies, and as a food resource for microorganisms. Microbial decomposition and physical fragmentation of leaves contribute fine particles to collector-gatherers. Leaves of some species (for example, Cottonwood) decompose rapidly and may be substantially degraded *in situ* rather than exported. Terrestrially derived fine particles enter the channel in overland flow associated with convective summer storms, and are incorporated in the sandy sediments upon flood recession. This is the main food of many invertebrates immediately following flash flooding (Gray 1980). It is clear, however, that accumulations of large organic particles (whole leaves) in desert streams are rare, as are the organisms equipped to use this material directly.

Primary Production

In addition to high insolation, many desert streams experience the long growing season, high temperatures, and ample dissolved nutrients requisite to high annual primary productivity. The point is obvious, but often overlooked—however conducive chemical and physical conditions may be, the machinery must be in place to permit photosynthesis. Instantaneous primary production on an areal basis is a function of chlorophyll *a* density (Busch and Fisher 1981). Algal standing crop varies, and floods are the primary agents of removal. One cannot predict primary production on a given date without knowing the algal standing crop which is, in turn, a partial function of elapsed time since disturbance by flooding. Since flooding is stochastic within a broad seasonal pattern, annual primary production will be a function of flood frequency and timing.

Instantaneous standing crop of algae can be quite high if measurements are made months after flooding. Busch and Fisher (1981) report mean chlorophyll *a* in Sycamore Creek during midsummer of 191 mg/m^2; however, distribution is patchy, and *Cladophora glomerata* stands may exceed 700 mg chl *a*/m^2 locally. Total biomass (largely algae) under mean and maximum conditions in Sycamore Creek is 268 and 427 g/m^2, respectively. These maximum values probably reflect an upper limit for benthic chlorophyll *a* and algal biomass in streams. Tecopa Bore, a small, spring-fed Mohave Desert stream which never floods, exhibits a maximum standing crop (again mostly algal) of 260 g/m^2 in late summer (Naiman 1976). Two important points should thus be emphasized: (1) desert streams probably support nearly as much algal biomass as is possible in lotic ecosystems; and (2) these high standing crops are not unusual, but can occur every year as long as interflood periods extend several months.

Primary productivity is high in desert streams where measurements have been made. Rattlesnake Springs, a Great Basin Desert stream, has an annual gross primary production (Pg) rate of 3.0 g O_2/m^2 day (Cushing and Wolf 1982). Summer Pg in Pinto Creek, Arizona, is 5.3 g O_2/m^2 d (Lewis and Gerking 1979) and in Sycamore Creek, 8.5 g O_2/m^2 d (Busch and Fisher 1981). Naiman's (1976) Tecopa Bore averaged 8.7 g O_2/m^2 d primary production annually and ranged from 3.1 g O_2/m^2 d in December to 12.9 g O_2/m^2 d in May. Daily rates for desert streams are high, but not remarkably so. Silver Springs, Florida, exceeds 20 g O_2/m^2 d on an annual basis (Odum 1957); however, this is an unusual situation with constant flow and temperature year round and with a large standing crop of vascular hydrophytes. On a daily basis, small desert streams are two to three times as productive as their unpolluted mesic counterparts. Annual productivity may be considerably higher in desert streams, due to the long growing season, warm temperatures, and long undisturbed periods between floods.

In the Sonoran Desert, winter rains and ensuing runoff are probably most critical in shaping annual primary production in that high flow may persist for several months, preventing rapid reestablishment of algae.

Summer rains are probably less important, for while floods remove virtually all photosynthesizers, flood recession is rapid and preflood chlorophyll density is regained in two to three weeks (Fisher et al. 1982).

ORGANIC MATTER UTILIZATION

The other side of the primary production coin is, of course, organic matter utilization. In many ways, less is known about degradative processes (estimated by ecosystem respiration) than accretive processes (Pg) in desert streams. For those desert systems described earlier, respiration is slightly less than gross primary production and the ratio of P to R exceeds one, characteristic of autotrophic ecosystems. This phenomenon will be addressed later, but for now, suffice it to say that most of what is produced is consumed. The desert stream is thus supported largely by *in situ* primary production, but who are the consumers of this material and what is their relative importance?

Fishes are relatively abundant in desert streams, especially in summer when ecosystem boundaries shrink due to gradual drying without proportional fish mortality. In Sycamore Creek, *Agosia chrysogaster* (longfin dace), a cyprinid omnivore and perhaps the most common fish in Sonoran desert streams, reaches a density of 50 g/m² or more. *Pantosteus clarki* (Gila mountain sucker), *Notropis lutrensis* (red shiner), and *Pimephales promelas* (fathead minnow) are, collectively, an order of magnitude less abundant. Feeding studies show *Agosia* and *Pantosteus* guts to contain large quantities of algae in addition to macroinvertebrates (Fisher et al. 1981, Shreiber and Minckley 1981). *Agosia* ingests large amounts of *Cladophora* and its diatom epiphytes. *Pantosteus* ingests mostly epilithic diatoms characteristic of riffle substrates. While we have not yet quantified the impact of these fishes on the algal assemblage of the system, it is interesting that these abundant and common fishes are, in large part, herbivorous.

Invertebrates of desert streams are primarily collector-gatherers which select food based on particle size rather than on origin. Eighty-five percent of the invertebrate fauna of Sycamore Creek is comprised of sediment-deposit feeding chironomids and mayflies (Gray 1980). These taxa consume particles roughly in proportion to their occurrence in the system. For example, immediately after floods, insect guts are packed with minute woody fragments evidently derived from the terrestrial watershed. Insects quickly switch to diatoms when they become numerous (three to seven days after flooding) and then to *Cladophora*-derived detritus after two to three weeks (Fisher et al. 1982). Of the one hundred or so macroinvertebrate species in Sycamore Creek, only a handful consume *Cladophora* alive. Several others, particularly beetles, hemipterans, and odonates, are predators, feeding largely on chironomids and mayflies, but occasionally taking small fishes as well.

In terms of energy flow, the macroinvertebrate community of desert streams is overwhelmingly dominated by fine particle feeders. Collectors are small, abundant (to $300,000/m^2$), and grow rapidly. The several mayfly and chironomid species present in Sycamore Creek complete their life cycle from egg to adult in seven to fourteen days at summer temperatures—far faster than similar taxa in mesic streams (Gray 1981). As a result, their turnover rate is enormous, with annual secondary production exceeding standing stock by sixty to seventyfold (two to fivefold is more typical of mesic stream faunas; Waters 1969). As a result of this rapid turnover, secondary production in Sycamore Creek is 135 g/m^2 yr, one of the highest rates reported for any stream invertebrate funa (Fisher and Gray 1983).

But the story does not end here. The collector-gatherers of Sycamore Creek have an exceedingly low assimilation efficiency (about 10%). Since 50% of assimilated energy is respired, every unit of growth (secondary production) requires twenty ingested units. We thus calculate that the collector community ingests four times its body weight per day, and since mean standing stock is 3.0 g/m^2, 12 g/m^2 is ingested daily by insects. Recall that primary production in this system averages about 8.5 g O_2/m^2 d! In one flood-recovery sequence, collector insects reached 10 g/m^2 and ingested nearly six times more material than was being produced. This is, of course, possible because much ingested material is passed through the gut relatively unchanged. Nonetheless, invertebrates turn over total organic matter every three days in this highly dynamic ecosystem. For some fractions, turnover is even higher. *Cladophora*, for example, is hardly consumed by invertebrates at all until after it dies and becomes detritus; thus, other organic components must turn over very rapidly to offset this large but relatively inactive pool.

These numbers document an extremely active invertebrate component in desert streams attributable to moderate standing stock, rapid growth, and low assimilation efficiency. Gray (1981) suggests the rapid life cycle is a life history adaptation to stochastic flash flooding characteristic of southwestern desert streams. Low assimilation efficiency may similarly be an adaptation to low-quality but abundant food. The metabolic "strategy" of individuals may be to shorten gut retention time, absorb only the most readily metabolizable components of the food, release fecal material to the environment where bacterial processing improves its quality once again (for example, by augmenting its organic nitrogen content), and then reingesting this microbe-fecal complex. It is well known that microbes condition detrital materials (leaves) in mesic streams and improve its quality as food for consumers (Petersen and Cummins 1974). This is a similar process involving fine particles and is enhanced by the rapid conditioning made possible by higher temperatures in streams of warm deserts. Still, this scenario must remain a hypothesis until it can be demonstrated that microbial conditioning of fine particles occurs at substantial rates in natural desert streams.

While insects are highly active in terms of ingestion of materials, only about 22% of total ecosystem respiration is attributed to this component (Fisher et al. 1982). A large part of the remainder is assignable to plants, and a probably minor fraction to fishes. While we have not quantified component respiration adequately enough to estimate microbial activity, there is reason to believe it substantial. First, macroinvertebrates are confined to the upper few centimeters of the sediment surface and are very rare deeper than 10 cm. Secondly, deep sediment cores (>10 cm) show high oxygen demand. Third, chamber respiration estimates (which include only the top 1–2 cm of sediment) consistently underestimate whole system respiration (as measured by upstream–downstream O_2 methods). We attribute this deep sediment oxygen demand to microbial processing of dissolved and particulate organic matter entrained in interstitial spaces. In a 30 m reach of Sycamore Creek where sandy sediments extend 42 cm below the stream bottom, hyporheic respiration was equivalent to surface respiration, the latter including all macroinvertebrates and all photosynthetic organisms (Grimm and Fisher 1984). This is especially striking because sediments are only 0.3% organic and appear to be clean washed sand. Secondly, oxygen demand of sediments is sufficient to deplete oxygen from saturation to zero mg/l in 3–4 h, yet interstitial samples consistently exhibited oxygen at 6–7 mg/l. Depletion of O_2 is prevented by rapid, thorough exchange of surface and interstitial water through these porous substrates. Dye studies indicate water flows through interstitial spaces at from 0.05 to 0.14 cm/s, with the direction of flow upward where the stream bottom is convex to the sky and downward where it is concave.

These data indicate that the hyporheic zone is an active component of desert stream metabolism. By implication, mesic stream studies should also include the hyporheic, but they seldom do. (Hyporheic exchanges in streams were first described in mesic trout streams not in deserts.) Our studies of this phenomenon dictate the use of three layer (water + sediment surface + hyporheic) models for stream ecosystems rather than the traditional two layers. To ignore deep sediment metabolism is to underestimate ecosystem respiration and to estimate P/R erroneously high. Our August 1982 studies in Sycamore Creek yielded a P/R of 1.9 without the deep sediment component and 0.9 with it. This obviously makes a great difference in attempting to judge whether a stream is autotrophic (P/R>1) or heterotrophic (P/R<1) overall. Desert streams, in fact all streams studied as two-layered systems, may be considerably less autotrophic than heretofore thought.

The autotrophy-heterotrophy question is an important one in stream ecology. Shaded forest streams are clearly heterotrophic with excess respiration supported by terrestrial inputs of organic matter. Autotrophy as a process may be important in a variety of streams, especially in deserts (Minshall 1978), but this is not to say these stream ecosystems are autotrophic (P/R>1). An autotrophic stream operating at steady state must export excess photosynthate to downstream reaches, reservoirs, or the floodplain. At the same time, purportedly autotrophic desert streams receive vast allochthonous inputs mostly as fine particles from the terrestrial watershed during flash flooding. This material is incorporated in sandy sediments as the flood recedes and provides a large reservoir of substrates for consumer respiration during interflood periods. If our data are general and desert stream P/R is near one, export of photosynthate is approximately offset by flood import of fine particles, and desert streams are neither autotrophic nor heterotrophic but are in balance with respect to organic matter.

It should be said, however, that to resolve a complete organic matter budget requires measurement of fluxes into and out of the system, most of which occur during catastrophic floods (Fisher and Minckley 1978). Because the organic matter budget of desert streams is so dominated by abiotic flooding events, little annual budget work has been or is likely to be done by biologists. This is doubly true of nutrient budgets.

NUTRIENT DYNAMICS

The study of watershed-level nutrient budgets has been a particularly promising theme in ecosystem ecology in the past two decades (Likens and Bormann 1977). In mesic watersheds, rare events are responsible for disproportionately large outputs—one November storm at Hubbard Brook accounted for 54% of the two-yr particulate output from a small watershed (Bormann et al. 1969). This situation is accentuated in the Sonoran Desert where runoff is rarer yet and is closely linked to convective summer thunderstorms. For example, 70% of the water yield from the Sycamore Creek watershed occurs during only 3% of the time in an average year, and nearly 30% of total runoff occurs in a single day (Fisher and Minckley 1978). To establish water budgets requires careful monitoring of rare events. Because nutrient concentrations increase greatly during floods, construction of nutrient budgets requires even more concentrated sampling. For example, suspended particulates in Sycamore Creek rose from 0.3 g/l prior to flooding to 55 g/l during a September flash flood peak. During this flood, water output and particulate concentration each increased two hundredfold for a total transport multiplier of 4×10^4 (Fisher and Minckley 1978). An adequate annual nutrient budget could be generated with very few samples—all of them of floodwater—yet the budget would tell us little of biotic control and regulation of nutrient cycling or of the influence of nutrient fluxes on aquatic biota. The biologically interesting interactions occur during typical low flow periods between floods—periods irrelevant to watershed-level budgets.

In smaller arid watersheds, the picture is even more dramatic. Small stream channels flow only in response to storms and only for a few hours per year. There is no stream biota; thus, the event is largely hydrologic and geochemical. Yet it is these small watersheds which route water to larger, permanent streams, or to aquifers that gradually release water to permanent streams or springs for months or years after a precipitation event.

We monitored chemistry during three consecutive summer storms on a small (0.65 ha), usually dry watershed in desert scrub near Apache Junction, Arizona (S. G. Fisher and N. B. Grimm, unpublished data). Both precipitation and water chemistry during those storms were variable, but several patterns emerged. While storms were intense, less than 25% of precipitation appeared in runoff (Table 6.1). Nutrient chemistry of precipitation and runoff were elevated, particularly nitrogen. Runoff concentrations exceeded precipitation by two to twenty-sixfold, yet only phosphorus and suspended solids exhibited net dissolved losses from the watershed. Most of the dissolved input via precipitation was retained. In spite of this, runoff from this typical headwater system was exceedingly high in nitrogen and phosphorus. None of this water flowed on the surface beyond 10 km from its source, but seeped into the sandy alluvial sediments of larger downstream channels—channels much smaller than permanent streams of the region. This runoff water recharges aquifers, including deep sand sediments in large channels such as Sycamore Creek. Water emerges and flows as a stream where bedrock or other unconformities force it to the surface (Figure 6.1). As bedrock falls away, water seeps again into subsurface storage. The point here is that water emerging at stream sources or springs has the chemistry of sheet or small channel flow and may have entered the watershed months (or years) earlier. In particular, nitrate-nitrogen is very high—a fact of great implication for

Table 6.1. Chemistry of precipitation (P) and runoff (RO) from a small first-order watershed near Apache Junction, Arizona. Storms generating runoff occurred on three successive days. Note that phosphorus and suspended solids (SS) exhibit net losses during the event but other constituents show net gains (precipitation input > runoff output). TDN = total dissolved nitrogen = nitrate + ammonium + dissolved organic N.

	Storm 1 (8/22)	Storm 2 (8/23)	Storm 3 (8/24)
Rainfall Duration (min)	35	40	11
Flow Duration (min)	36	36	22
Maximum Discharge (1/s)	27.2	20	10
Percent Runoff	25	24	10

			Chemistry						
	P	RO	RO/P	P	RO	RO/P	P	RO	RO/P
H_2O (mm)	14	3.5	.25	11	2.6	.24	5	.52	.10
Cl (mg/l)	1	4.5	4.5	3.4	3.7	1.1	2.3	6.7	2.9
PO_4-P (mg/l)	.06	.44	7.6[+]	.06	.30	5.5[+]	.016	.42	26[+]
NO_3-N (mg/l)	.52	1.01	1.9	.65	1.12	1.7	.34	2.8	8.3
TDN (mg/l)	1.31	2.7	2.1	1.75	2.16	1.23	1.07	3.44	3.21
SS (g/l)	T	1.46	*[+]	T	.25	*[+]	T	.47	*[+]

T = trace amount present but not measured.
*Output much higher than input.
[+]Represents net loss from watershed.

nutrient cycling in permanent desert streams. Phosphorus is high in headwater runoff (Table 6.1) but decreases about tenfold before emerging in springs and streams and exhibits less variation between sites than does nitrogen (Grimm et al. 1981).

Our recently completed survey of surface waters at 196 stream and spring sites in the Southwest reveals that nitrate-nitrogen concentrations in spring/source water and in flood waters are significantly higher than in free-flowing streams and rivers of the region, yet spring and floodwater nitrogen values are not significantly different from each other. Phosphate-phosphorus concentrations, on the other hand, show no significant differences among system types, time of year or flood stage (Table 6.2). As a result, the ratio of nitrate-nitrogen to phosphate-phosphorus (N:P) is significantly higher at springs, stream sources, and in floodwater than in

Stuart G. Fisher

Table 6.2. Mean nitrate–N and soluble reactive phosphorus (SRP) concentrations for 196 stream sites in Arizona.

System Type	n =	NO$_3$–N mean mg/l	STD DEV	SRP mean mg/l	STD DEV	NO$_3$–N:SRP (atomic)
Summer low flow stream	92	.068[1]	.162	.039	.059	3.9[2]
Winter high flow stream	14	.118	.122	.053	.057	4.9
Floodwater	34	.414	.608	.049	.046	18.7
Springs	56	.491	.836	.037	.050	29.4
All Systems	196	.252	.558	.041	.054	13.6

[1]Significantly lower than both floodwaters and springs ($p < 0.001$).
[2]Significantly lower than springs ($p < 0.01$).
No other differences among NO$_3$–N, SRP, or N:P are significant.

free-flowing streams. The downward adjustment in N:P as water flows downstream from stream sources is wholly attributable to nitrate decline. Phosphorus averages 0.041 mg/l and varies little from place to place.

Grimm et al. (1981) have shown that the downstream decline in nitrate is largely due to algal uptake during net photosynthesis. We have yet to determine the factors responsible for control of phosphate-phosphorus. Phosphorus is certainly taken up during algal production, yet no longitudinal concentration decline occurs. It is striking that the phosphorus levels we see in many southwestern streams are near the equilibrium concentration for calcium phosphate; thus, phosphorus may be controlled simply by solubility (Stumm and Morgan 1981).

The net effect of these downstream changes is to reduce atomic N:P from greater than 15:1, indicating potential phosphorus limitation, to less than 15:1, indicating potential nitrogen limitation. Most desert streams are short in nitrogen relative to phosphorus, and in highly productive situations nitrate-nitrogen drops below our detection limit (that is, <0.001 mg/l) and may actually limit net production. While we have yet to confirm nitrogen limitation experimentally, the frequent ascension of nitrogen-fixing blue-green algae in nitrogen-poor waters supports this hypothesis.

In summary, rainwater, floodwater, and stream source water are high in nitrogen and low in phosphorus, but the biota of desert streams lower nitrogen (not phosphorus) to the point where potential nitrogen limitation occurs. Needless to say, this water filling lakes and reservoirs will also create a situation of nitrogen limitation or will foster the dominance of blue-green algae. In contrast to many aquatic ecosystems of other regions, southwestern ecosystems are most probably nitrogen, not phosphorus, limited.

SUCCESSION IN DESERT STREAMS

Desert streams draining large watersheds provide an excellent opportunity to test successional concepts in running waters. Base flow only gradually declines in summer and resetting flash floods are infrequent (two to nine per year in Sycamore Creek). As a result, long, relatively stable interflood periods are available for study of temporal succession at a single site (Figure 6.2). Flash floods are devastating, removing most of the stream biota (except fishes), yet they recede rapidly, leaving a physically restored channel devoid of biota. Recovery following flooding, reported in detail elsewhere (Fisher et al. 1982), is rapid, largely because most organisms are vagile, small, and develop rapidly (Figure 6.3).

Diatoms are the first algal colonizers, followed by filamentous greens (for example, *Cladophora glomerata*) and later by bluegreens. Productivity is high and 100 g/m² algal standing crop is achieved in two weeks. Both mayflies and dipterans are devastated by flooding but recover rapidly, thanks to an immune aerial adult component and rapid development of immatures. Invertebrate biomass is thus restored to preflood levels within four weeks. Ecosystem metabolism also recovers rapidly in an asymptotic fashion. Five days after flood recession, gross primary production exceeds community respiration (Figure 6.4).

Succession in Sycamore Creek varies considerably from the general features of succession proposed by Odum (1969). Differences are most prominent in features influenced greatly by streamflow and organic matter export (for example, P and R do not converge, excess P is exported). Communities also remain composed of small, fast organisms contrary to Odum's prediction that an increase in size through succession should occur. Apparently, large organisms (with slower life cycles) would be selected against in an ecosystem subject to stochastic, devastating flooding events.

Had stream ecology originated as a science in arid regions, succession would probably be a major conceptual organizer in lotic studies, as it is in terrestrial ecosystems worldwide. But it did not, and succession is only a minor element of our collective view of the generalized stream ecosystem. Why is this? Two possible reasons come to mind. First, floods in mesic streams may be thought to have a substantial effect on the biota,

A. MESIC STREAM (flood-immune biota)

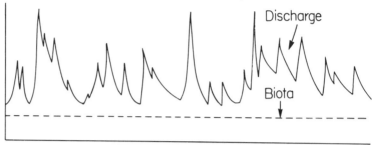

B. MESIC STREAM (flood-sensitive biota)

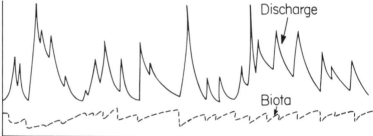

C. DESERT STREAM

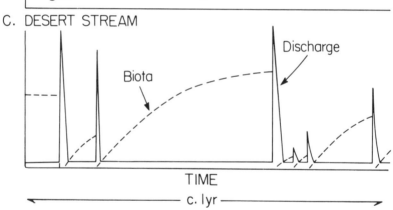

TIME

c. lyr

Figure 6.2 Hypothetical response of stream biota to flooding events. A. Mesic stream with biota unaffected by subannual spates. B. Mesic stream model where biota is affected by flooding but interflood period is too short to permit detectable change. C. Desert stream where infrequent floods decimate the biota and long interflood periods permit substantial recovery trajectories (succession).

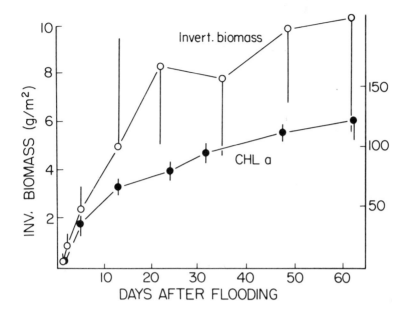

Figure 6.3 Recovery of Sycamore Creek biota after a summer flash flood. Invertebrate biomass expressed as dry mass. Chlorophyll *a* is exclusively algal. Flood removed >95% of the biota. Preflood levels were attained in two to three weeks.

but occur so frequently that interflood periods may be too short to resolve community change in time (Figure 6.2b). Alternatively, mesic faunas and floras may be considered immune to flooding and show little response to subannual spates (Figure 6.2a). The true case probably lies between these, and shifts depending upon the biotic group or collective property under consideration. The insect fauna of trout streams tolerates moderate flooding with little consequence as evidenced by long life cycles and fairly constant year-to-year community composition. Algae and microinvertebrates, especially those of sandy substrates, are undoubtedly decimated by spates and recover slowly. A stream ecologist working on mayfly communities may execute a rigid monthly sampling regime irrespective of flooding and suffer little. However, monthly measures of primary production taken on the same schedule may defy interpretation. So it matters what questions are asked. Most will agree, however, that prediction of state variables, even for mesic streams, is tenuous in ignorance of disturbance magnitude and frequency.

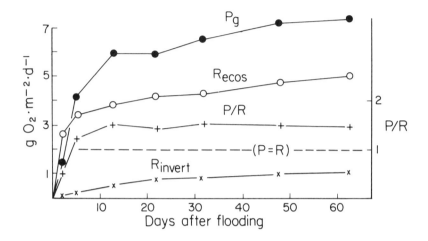

Figure 6.4 Recovery of Sycamore Creek ecosystem metabolism after a summer flash flood. Preflood rates were attained in two weeks. Note that the system achieved autotrophy (P>R) within 5 d. R invert = respiration attributed to macroinvertebrates.

Part of the explanation for the nonsuccessional view of streams may stem from the evolutionary history of the biota. Predominant species in torrential streams have evolved in this context and could be considered pioneer species in others. We should not be surprised that taxa characteristic of moderate flows, typifying late successional stages in desert streams, do not exist in mountain brooks. An ecosystem in which the entire species pool consists of "pioneer" species is unlikely to exhibit temporal succession. Of course, all mesic streams are neither torrential nor trout streams. It is possible that the utility of the successional concept simply has not yet been recognized by stream ecologists elsewhere. Desert stream studies suggest it to be a strong, potentially insightful concept.

Finally, a word should be said about longitudinal succession, a concept deeply ingrained in lotic ecology, usually in the form of river zonation studies, but more recently as the river continuum concept (RCC; Vannote et al. 1980). Both concepts are biological, dealing predominantly with the structure of communities from headwater brooks to large rivers. The RCC goes farther in including productivity and organic matter processing among dependent variables. For example, headwater streams are dominated by allochthonous litter and shredders, while fine-sediment organic matter and associated benthic consumers, along with an active suspended organic matter–plankton community, characterize large rivers. The RCC promises to greatly influence stream ecology, especially when research is directed toward testing hypotheses explaining these observed patterns. Predominant among hypothesized causes of longitudinal pattern are physical changes downstream (slope, velocity, substrate, depth) and longitudinal biologic influence (for example, upstream organisms reduce particle size, alter water chemistry, and excrete waste products, all of which affect downstream communities).

Desert streams may help resolve RCC causation in several ways, not the least of which is to extend its generality to nonforested areas. It is no surprise that longitudinal patterns in desert streams differ from those in New England. The challenge is to frame the explanatory hypothesis sufficiently broadly to incorporate both. Desert streams (and semiarid grassland streams) may help in this endeavor by providing natural experiments. An isolated reach of Sycamore Creek provides an opportunity to examine longitudinal change in a few hundred meters. For example, do upstream algae depress dissolved nutrients sufficiently to alter the productivity and community composition of downstream algae? Preliminary observations of concrete canals in central Arizona suggest longitudinal biologic change can occur *without* attendant changes in channel morphometry, and with no tributary inputs (Marsh and Fisher, unpublished). Desert drainages may also provide a series of unconnected reaches in the same drainage, each in a different geomorphic setting, yet unconnected through surface water flow.

I emphasize the research utility of streams in deserts to make this final point. Yes, desert streams (and other desert ecosystems) are different, sometimes strikingly, from their analogues elsewhere. That deserts cover 25% of the global land surface argues strongly for continued research to describe their diversity and uniqueness. But a far greater contribution will be made if desert research sharpens and clarifies ecosystem principles which also apply elsewhere. To regard desert streams as exceptions is to admit that the rule is parochial.

REFERENCES

Anderson, N. H., and K. W. Cummins. 1979. Influences of diet on the life histories of aquatic insects. Journal of the Fisheries Research Board of Canada 36:335–342.
Bilby, R. E., and G. E. Likens. 1980. Importance of organic debris dams in the structure and function of stream ecosystems. Ecology 61:1107–1113.

Bormann, F. H., G. E. Likens, and J. S. Eaton. 1969. Biotic regulation of particulate and solution losses from a forest ecosystem. BioScience 19:600–610.

Busch, D. E., and S. G. Fisher. 1981. Metabolism of a desert stream. Freshwater Biology 11:301–307.

Cummins, K. W. 1974. Structure and function of stream ecosystems. BioScience 24:631–641.

Cushing, C. E., and E. G. Wolf. 1982. Organic energy budget of Rattlesnake Springs, Washington. American Midland Naturalist 107:404–407.

Fisher, S. G. 1977. Organic matter processing by a stream-segment ecosystem: Fort River, Massachusetts, U.S.A. International Review of Hydrobology 62:701–727.

Fisher, S. G., D. E. Busch, and N. B. Grimm. 1981. Diel feeding chronologies in two Sonoran Desert stream fishes, *Agosia chrysogaster* (Cyprinidae) and *Pantosteus clarki* (Catostomidae). Southwestern Naturalist 26:31–36.

Fisher, S. G., and L. J. Gray. 1983. Secondary production and organic matter processing by collector macroinvertebrates in a desert stream. Ecology 64:1217–1224.

Fisher, S. G., L. J. Gray, N. B. Grimm, and D. E. Busch. 1982. Temporal succession in a desert stream ecosystem following flash flooding. Ecological Monographs 52:93–110.

Fisher, S. G., and G. E. Likens. 1973. Energy flow in Bear Brook, New Hampshire: an integrative approach to stream ecosystem metabolism. Ecological Monographs 43:421–439.

Fisher, S. G., and W. L. Minckley. 1978. Chemical characteristics of a desert stream in flash flood. Journal of Arid Environments 1:25–33.

Gray, L. J. 1980. Recolonization on pathways and community development of desert stream macroinvertebrates. Ph.D. dissertation. Arizona State University, Tempe.

Gray, L. J. 1981. Species composition and life histories of aquatic insects in a lowland Sonoran Desert stream. American Midland Naturalist 106:229–242.

Grimm, N. B., and S. G. Fisher. 1984. Exchange between interstitial and surface water: implications for stream metabolism and nutrient cycling. Hydrobiologia 3:219–228.

Grimm, N. B., S. G. Fisher, and W. L. Minckley. 1981. Nitrogen and phosphorus dynamics in hot desert streams of Southwestern U.S.A. Hydrobiologia 83:303–312.

Keller, E. A., and F. J. Swanson. 1979. Effects of large organic material on channel form and fluvial process. Earth Surface Processes 4:361–380.

Lewis, M. A., and S. D. Gerking. 1979. Primary productivity in a polluted intermittent desert stream. American Midland Naturalist 102:172–174.

Likens, G. E., and F. H. Bormann. 1977. Biogeochemistry of a forested ecosystem. New York: Springer-Verlag.

Mathews, C. P., and A. Kowalczewski. 1969. The disappearance of leaf litter and its contribution to production in the River Thames. Journal of Ecology 57:543–552.

Minshall, G. W. 1978. Autotrophy in stream ecosystems. BioScience 28:767–771.

Naiman, R. J. 1976. Primary production, standing stock and export of organic matter in a Mojave Desert thermal stream. Limnology and Oceanography 21:60–73.

Naiman, R. J., and J. R. Sedell. 1979. Benthic organic matter as a function of stream order in Oregon. Archives of Hydrobiology 87:404–422.

Newbold, J. D., J. W. Elwood, R. V. O'Neill, and W. Van Winkle. 1981. Measuring nutrient spiralling in streams. Canadian Journal of Fisheries and Aquatic Sciences 38:860–863.

Odum, H. T. 1957. Trophic structure and productivity of Silver Springs, Florida. Ecological Monographs 27:55–112.

Odum, E. P. 1969. The strategy of ecosystem development. Science 164:262–270.

Petersen, R. C., and K. W. Cummins. 1974. Leaf processing in a woodland stream. Freshwater Biology 4:343–368.

Rounick, J. S., M. J. Winterbourn, and G. L. Lyon. 1982. Differential utilization of allochthonous and autochthonous inputs by aquatic invertebrates in some New Zealand streams: a stable carbon isotope study. Oikos 39:191–198.

Schreiber, D. C., and W. L. Minckley. 1981. Feeding interrelations of native fishes in a Sonoran Desert stream. The Great Basin Naturalist 41(4):409–426.

Strahler, A. N. 1957. Quantitative analysis of watershed geomorphology. Transcripts of the American Geophysical Union 38:913–920.

Stumm, W., and J. J. Morgan. 1981. Aquatic chemistry. John Wiley and Sons, New York.

Suberkropp, K., G. L. Codshalk, and M. J. Klug. 1976. Changes in the chemical composition of leaves during processing in a woodland stream. Ecology 57:720–727.

Thomsen, B. W., and H. H. Schumann. 1968. The Sycamore Creek watershed, Maricopa County, Arizona. Water Supply Paper 1861. U.S. Geological Survey, Washington, D.C.

Vannote, R. L., G. W. Minshall, K. W. Cummins, J. R. Sedel, and C. E. Cushing. 1980. The river continuum concept. Canadian Journal of Fisheries and Aquatic Sciences 37:130–137.

Waters, T. F. 1969. The turnover ratio in production ecology of freshwater invertebrates. American Naturalist 103:173–185.

Webster, J. R. 1975. Analysis of potassium and calcium dynamics in stream ecosystems on three southern Appalachian watersheds of contrasting vegetation. Ph.D. dissertation, University of Georgia.